Activating Bodhicitta:

The Awakening Mind

&

Meditation on Compassion

Published in commemoration of the 2550th Mahaparinirvana anniversary of Buddha Shakyamuni

Activating Bodhicitta:
The Awakening Mind
&
Meditation on Compassion

by

His Holiness the
Fourteenth Dalai Lama

LIBRARY OF TIBETAN WORKS & ARCHIVES

First Print: 1979 under the title *Aryasura's Aspiration and a Meditation on Compassion*
Second edition: 2006

ISBN: 81-86470-52-2

Published by the Library of Tibetan Works and Archives, Dharamsala, and printed at Indraprastha Press (CBT), 4 BahadurShah Zafar Marg, New Delhi - 110 002

Content

Translator's Note

Then following exposition by His Holiness the present Dalai Lama on developing great compassion and activating the awakening mind is adapted from a discourse on Nāgārjuna's *Precious Garland* (Rin-chen-'phreng-ba; Ratnamālā) given in February, 1975, in the main temple at Thekchen Choling, Upper Dharamsala, India. The translation was undertaken by Gonsar Rinpoche at the request of the Swiss nun, Mme. Ansermet, was transcribed by Brian Grabia and prepared and written in its present form by Brian Beresford at the Translation Bureau of the L.T.W.A. in June/July, 1978.

Introduction

The precious awakening mind of bodhicitta, which cherishes other sentient beings instead of oneself, is the trunk of the Bodhisattva's practice—the path of the Great Vehicle. It is the base and foundation of all the activities of an Awakening Warrior, a Bodhisattva—activities which are, for ordinary beings, even difficult to rejoice in. This awakening mind transforms all one's wholesome actions into a catalyst for the attainment of Buddhahood. This is an ultimate state of mind that will enable us to accomplish our own welfare as well as that of all other sentient beings. For these reasons the great beings and saints keep this altruistic mind of bodhicitta as their essential practice.

Although this mind is something which is difficult to activate, it is absolutely necessary for us to make an effort to generate it within ourselves. At this time we are very fortunate, not just to have a human birth, but to have come in contact with the Mahāyāna Dharma—the teachings of the Great Vehicle's path. We have the opportunity to emulate the practices of the great beings of the past. Even to hear one word about bodhicitta is most fortunate and this is absolutely true because there is no more virtuous mind than bodhicitta. There is no more powerful mind than bodhicitta. There is no more joyous mind than bodhicitta. For the accomplishment of one's own ultimate purpose, the awakening mind is supreme, and to accomplish the purpose of all other living beings there is nothing superior to bodhicitta. The awakening mind is the unsurpassable way to collect merit. To purify obstacles bodhicitta is supreme. For protection from interferences bodhicitta is supreme. It is the unique, all-encompassing method. Every kind of ordinary and supra-mundane power can be accomplished through bodhicitta. Thus, it is absolutely precious.

Even though we personally may find difficulty in immediate and thorough generation of such a mind, we should at least direct our thoughts towards it. To train our mind in such an ultimately altruistic manner from the very beginning of our practice of Dharma is vitally important. From the very initial stages of spiritual practice when we meditate on turning away from clinging to this lifetime, and also clinging to the next, we should already be acquainting ourselves with the awakening mind. Even if we practice one session of meditation on the path in common with the being of smallest aptitude (such as contemplations on impermanence, death, renunciation and so forth), to begin this with the altruistic aspiration to attain complete realization for the benefit of all, will already make a difference in our practice, helping to shorten the path. At least we should believe in it, for not only does it help to shorten the path, it also channels one's practice along the right path without letting it go astray into lesser aspirations.

No matter what spiritual practice we do as Mahāyāna Buddhists, they all begin with going for refuge in the Three Rare and Supreme Jewels and the activation of the awakening mind. This means not merely repeating the words but integrating their meaning into our mind. Thinking deeply about the implication behind the prayers is what brings the best result. This is very important. Now, although our bodhicitta is at the level of wishing and praying, this is not enough. We must train our mind in it for a long time and then enhance it within ourselves. In order to do this, we should first know the teachings which contain the instructions on how to activate it. These can be found briefly in the great work of Nāgārjuna entitled *The Precious Garland*, which explains both the vast practices of the Bodhisattva and the profound view of emptiness.

From this text, the methods of obtaining a high rebirth status and the definite goodness of the state beyond sorrow, or nīrvāṇa, have been explained in the first chapter. This included an explanation of the profound view of emptiness as well as details of practices relating to the observance of the law of cause and effect. This second chapter explaining the interrelationship of high status and definite goodness has so far covered some teaching in connection with the attainment of high status. Now Nāgārjuna devotes one and a half stanzas to the essence of the Mahāyāna path—all-encompassing compassion and the altruistic motivation of the awakening mind. He states (174b &175):

> If you and the world wish to attain
> unsurpassable full awakening,
> the root is the awakening mind
> that should be as stable as Meru, king of the mountains:
> (comprised of) compassion extending to all quarters,
> and discriminating wisdom which does not rely on duality.

Taking into consideration the aspirations of oneself and all other living beings, whosoever wishes to attain the ultimate enlightenment of Buddhahood should understand that the root and source of such an attainment is the precious bodhicitta, the mind awakening to its fullest potential for the sake of oneself and others. Therefore, this precious awakening mind must be activated, developed, enhanced and stabilized till it is as steady as the king of mountains, Mount Meru. In order to activate such a mind, we need to have developed great compassion since the wish to alleviate all sentient beings from their miseries is the root of bodhicitta. We should have this from the depths of our heart, as if it were nailed there. Such compassion is not merely concerned with a few sentient beings such as friends and relatives, but extends up to the limits of the cosmos, in all directions and towards all beings throughout space. Moreover, to realize enlightenment we need the discriminating wisdom which does not adhere to the duality of the two extreme viewpoints—the nihilistic belief in non-existence and the materialistic belief in the unchanging inherent identity of all phenomena. This is the discriminating intelligence which perfectly analyses the implication of the "Middle Way", or madhyamaka.

These three—the awakening mind of bodhicitta, compassion and discriminating wisdom—should be totally integrated. The method (including bodhicitta and compassion) and the wisdom (of the meaning of emptiness) must be combined, integrated and enhanced.

From this stanza in the *Precious Garland*, Nāgārjuna begins the actual path of the Great Vehicle, the preceding sections having dealt with what is in common with the path of the Lesser Vehicle, or Hīnayāna. From here onwards comes the very precious explanation of the awakening mind and how to activate it. The awakening mind is so worthwhile, precious and wholesome that it is beneficial to develop it even though it may take countless lifetimes and hundreds of aeons. Bodhicitta is a tidal wave on the ocean of practices to Buddhahood. Even temporarily, the power of the awakening mind can easily overcome whatever difficulties and hardships we may face so that we are not overwhelmed and discouraged. So indeed it is the sole, universal panacea.

The Seven Instructions of Causes and Their Effect

How should we activate the awakening mind? Although there are many excellent methods that have been explained by the learned masters of the past, two of the most well-known are: (1) transforming one's thoughts through the seven instructions of six causes and their effect; and (2) transforming one's thoughts by exchanging oneself with others.

I. Equanimity: An Unbiased Attitude

According to the first method, in order to generate a strong aspiration, a strong wish from the very depths of our heart that is not vague or superficial, to work for the benefit of all sentient beings, it is first essential to make all sentient beings appear equally dear to our thoughts. To gain that impression we must make all the bumps on our mind even. At present we hold many contradictory and biased attitudes towards sentient beings whereas such attitudes are unnatural and unreasonable. We maintain these different biases because of some reason that we believe in such as, "This person has helped me, whereas this one has harmed me. Therefore I should feel attraction for the former and aversion for the latter." This is our usual justification for preferences.

However, as far as the help and harm that beings bestow upon us, both are equally true. Those who help us much at present have no doubt harmed us very much in the past, and those who harm us now have helped us before. To have intense attraction towards one being and aversion to another merely because of the present situation is utterly wrong. Since the helper now has harmed us before and the harmer now has helped us in the past, the sum total of both benefit and injury is equal. As is mentioned in the ancient stories, someone who previously was one's most bitter enemy was born as one's cherished son, and those who have given one life, one's parents, were born as a dog or some other animal one is harming. As is said in the scriptures;

> She eats the flesh of the father and abuses the mother while cradling the most bitter enemy in her lap.

The specific story relating to this account is that at one time there was a widow and her son. The mother of this woman had died and was reborn as a family dog; her father had also died and was born as a fish in a nearby river, and the very enemy who had murdered her in a previous life had been born as her son whom she held affectionately in her arms. This she did while eating the flesh of her very own father, who had been a fisherman and was born as a fish. At the same time, the dog, who had been her mother, chewed the bones of the fish of her husband. Furthermore, the woman constantly kicked and abused the dog who was her mother while cradling her former enemy in her lap. This family was perceived through the clairvoyant powers of the great Arhat Śāriputra who laughed and said:

> She eats the flesh of the father, scolds the dog, her mother, keeps dearly her karmic enemy on her lap while her mother gnaws the bones of her husband. Such occurrences in the wheel of existence are most amusing.

Thus there is no certainty of friend or enemy. In fact, they have equally harmed and helped us, so to hold onto such a biased attitude is not valid at all.

To apply this to your meditational practice, you should visualize three beings in front of you: a friend, an enemy and a stranger. Then imagine the enemy, directly in front of you, abusing and provoking you. If you think about this with someone you really consider as your enemy, it will suddenly produce agitation in your mind and thus hatred and aversion will arise. Then reflect on the friend who is very pleasant and is praising you with kind words. Immediately it will bring a measure of pleasure in your mind. Once you visualize and imagine in this way, automatically it will cause a feeling of closeness towards the friend to arise, an unpleasant feeling of aversion to the enemy, and a feeling of complete indifference for the stranger.

Then you should think, "This is absolutely ridiculous! Because of just a few words and actions I create all this agitation in my mind. This is complete nonsense." If we change these people's places, making the enemy a friend and so forth, then again our feelings change with this different approach. In this way we should realize that they, as enemies, friends or strangers, become completely essenceless and certainly not worthy of such intense discrimination, feeling attracted to one while hating another.

In this way, beginning with three people, we then expand our vision and train our mind away from bias until we are able to apply an even attitude to all sentient beings. After actualizing such equanimity we must relate to all sentient beings as our mothers.

II. Awareness of Mother Sentient Beings

Because we have taken countless births and have required a mother to give birth to us each time, and because the mind has been passing from one lifetime to the next from beginningless time, there are no beings who have not been our mother at some stage or other. Not only have they been our mothers, they have also been our friends, wives, husbands, lovers, relatives and so on. This is definite. Therefore, they all, in the capacity as mothers, friends and relatives, have protected us and have helped us with their kindness. Over all these times when every sentient being has been our mother or father, they have shown us the same kindness as have our parents of this present life. Although it may be possible that there are people who are hated by their mother, generally a mother's kindness and compassion towards her child is beyond comprehension.

Most mothers, for instance, even though they may have such a naughty child that people nearby become very annoyed and think "What is the use of such a child?" are never really aggravated. When a child is born, even though it is so little and weak, helpless and without any ability of its own, still the mother holds it as if she has found a precious treasure. Without any hesitation she would prefer herself to be ill or to die rather than have her child being ill and dying. Later on in life, even though she feels it is a pity to spend all the wealth and possessions she has accumulated on herself, if her child were to do so, even recklessly, she feels it is not wrong and may even rejoice in the child enjoying itself. In short, a mother tries to help and benefit her child as much as she can with all her ability and strength.

We have survived because our mother, with her love and affection, has so preciously and dearly protected us for days, weeks, months and years, until we can stand on our own two feet. If our mother had not nurtured and sheltered us, we should never have gained this opportunity to practice Dharma and have the freedoms we have.

III. Recollecting Their Kindness

Each time sentient beings have been our mother they have shown us the same kindness, and this holds true for mothers in the animal kingdom as much as in the world of mankind. Even insects mother their offspring and rear them with all their ability. To really think about this is so touching and heart-warming that it can make one's hair stand on end.

It is very moving the way mother birds, for example, rear their young. High on the walls of the Potala in Lhasa wild ducks would make their nests. When the young were being raised the mother would pluck her own feathers, becoming cold and weak, in order to line the nest for her offspring. When the time came for the ducklings to leave the nest, the parents had to throw them out so that they fell many stories before reaching the ground. This knocked them unconscious, leaving them prey to the attacks of hawks and crows. They would try to run and fly but often would be carried away. The parents, although helpless against such foes, tried as much as they could to protect their young. They walked around them, which was as much as they could do, putting themselves in danger, and gradually tried to lead them to the safety of the lake.

Not only human mothers, but all mothers down to the smallest insect strive to give all they can to their offspring. Therefore, once we have transformed our negative attitudes of intense attachment, hatred or total indifference towards others into an even, unbiased state of equanimity, we can meditate deeply on the recognition of all beings as our mothers. As it is said:

> In the ground of equanimity,
> moistened with the water of love,
> the seed of compassion is constantly sown
> giving rise to the ultimate fruit from
> the flourishing tree of the awakening mind.

Just how precious sentient beings are will be understood from the depths of our hearts by an honest investigation of the kindnesses they have rendered us.

IV. Repaying Their Kindness

Furthermore, we must think about the present situation of all these mother sentient beings who have been so kind to us in the past. What is that situation? It is that they are extremely ignorant about unwholesome actions that should be abandoned and virtuous ones that should be practiced. Yet they are not just ignorant of this fact, they also lack proper guidance to show them how to discriminate between right and wrong. If, for instance, by some accident they are fortunate enough to be on a safe path, there is still hope. Yet they are actually walking on the edge of a very dangerous precipice. Although they always wish for happiness, they are totally ignorant of how to assemble its causes. They wish to be free of suffering yet are constantly accumulating its causes. As Śāntideva has said in the *Venturing into the Bodhisattva's Way of Life* (byang-chub-sems-dpa'-spyod-pa-la-'jug-pa; Bodhisattva- caryāvatāra):

To be rid of misery we have the wish,
yet to misery itself we actually run.
Happiness we desire yet, through ignorance,
we destroy our own happiness like an enemy.

Like this, all beings' actions completely contradict their aspirations.

Now since all sentient beings have been extremely kind to us through or infinite lifetimes, we should endeavor to repay their kindness. To do otherwise, to remain quite unconcerned about their welfare and to remain totally preoccupied with our own benefit is actually very callous, inconsiderate and unkind. Even in an ordinary matter, if a blind person were helplessly stumbling along the edge of a cliff, anyone would come to his aid. To do otherwise would be considered bad and selfish. In the same way, all these sentient beings without any spiritual guide are blindly wandering along the cliff of transitory existence, their eye of wisdom blinded by lack of discriminating intelligence. They wish for happiness yet lack the causes. They wish to be free from suffering but have no idea what should be abandoned. They are in a very grave situation indeed. How can we ignore them and leave them like this? We must be concerned for their welfare and work as much as we can for the benefit of others.

V. Immaculate Love

Also, it is not sufficient for them to obtain just a temporary alleviation of their misery, a transitory happiness that soon will pass. We should reflect as it has been said in the Three Principals of the Path (Lam-gtso-rnam-gsum) by Tsong-kha-pa (stanzas 7 and 8):

Beings are continually carried away by the violent force
of the four rivers (of suffering);
they are tightly chained by the hard-to-avoid bonds of
karmic activity;
they are trapped in the iron mesh of ego-grasping;
they are enveloped in the gloom of ignorance.

Continually and endlessly they are tormented by the
three sufferings
in the boundless births of transitory existence.
Reflect upon the natural inclination of all mother beings
for states such as this, then kindly do generate the
awakening mind.

Since that is the true condition of all sentient beings, we must endeavor to release them from such anguish and misery and to establish them in a state of permanent happiness. In this way, by reflecting very deeply on the actual situation of all creatures, we generate compassion and pure love. Such a mind of compassion which wholeheartedly wishes for their immediate separation from suffering, will lead to the supreme intention to take the whole responsibility for that upon oneself.

VI. The Exceptional Thought

"By myself, I will take on the complete responsibility of making it possible for all beings to be free from all suffering and to be endowed with all joy and happiness." Once this supreme wish has been wholeheartedly generated, if we are asked whether we are really capable of doing this, we will realize that although we may try our best from now on and pray and so forth for the benefit of sentient beings, it remains merely a virtuous state of mind. We cannot really do as we may say or wish. Even if we pray, "May I attain the eye of wisdom, the psychic clairvoyances, the power of skillful speech, patience and other such qualities so that I can help others to the fullest extent," and we lack those qualities, this aspiration is no more than a wholesome state of mind.

The only one who is fully capable and totally ready to help in every way is a Fully Awakened Being—a Buddha. So long as ordinary beings are ready and receptive from their side for the help of a Fully Awakened Being, there will be no difficulty from the side of a Buddha to impart such ultimate help. Since the Awakened Beings are ready, we should be receptive. However, even the great Arhats who have eliminated all distrubing emotions and who have realized emptiness are incapable of fulfilling such wishes. They can lead others up to the stage they have attained but they cannot lead sentient beings to the ultimate stage, completely free from all traces of obscuration and suffering and totally endowed with happiness and virtues. Ultimately only a Buddha can help sentient beings.

VII. The Precious Awakening Mind

With this understanding, which is the result of the six previous instructions, we should generate an intense desire to attain the goal of Buddhahood just as a tool to help all sentient beings, since we realize that to do so is the best method, the best tool for accomplishing the ultimate welfare of oneself and others. Such a desire must be generated from the very depths of our heart. In the same way as is said in the Three Principals of the Path (stanza 5) concerning renunciation:

> When, through transforming the mind,
> desire for the perfections of cyclic existence
> does not arise for even a moment,
> When both day and night the mind yearns for
> liberation,
> at that time renunciation is born.

When the aspiration for full awakening for the benefit of all sentient beings arises in us spontaneously—all the time, day and night, in all our actions, whether walking or resting, eating or working—when these two wishes (to attain Buddhahood and to help sentient beings) arise together, the awakening mind, bodhicitta, is beginning to crystallize.

Exchanging Oneself with Others

The development of bodhicitta through the practice of exchanging oneself with others is stressed in the teachings of Nāgārjuna. For example, although the practice of transforming one's thoughts for activating the awakening mind is not explained in great detail in the *Precious Garland*, at the end of the text it says (stanza 484):

> May their sins ripen for me
> And all my virtues for them.

In Śāntideva's *Venturing into the Bodhisattva's Way of Life* this practice is explained in great detail in the eighth chapter on the topic of meditative concentration. Also, Maitreya, as transmitted to Asaṅga, has explained the exchanging of oneself with others in the *Ornament for the Mahāyāna Scriptures* (Mdo-sde-rgyan; Mahāyānasūtralaṅkara).

All these great masters explain that, to activate the awakening mind, excellent concentration is required, so we should first live in solitude, free from all external distractions and internal wanderings of the mind. Once that is obtained, one should begin by practicing meditation upon equality between oneself and others. Only then do we enter the real practice.

I. The Equality of Others

Oneself and all other beings are completely equal in wishing for happiness and for freedom from misery. However, we all constantly hold onto the concept of "I", "I" as though it were something to be treasured. Nevertheless, we do have every right to properly accumulate happiness and to abandon suffering. Just as we have these rights and wishes so do all other sentient beings, too including celestial beings. Thus the Dharmic practice of exchanging oneself with others or, in other words, putting oneself in the position of others and treating them as one would oneself, is a practice that takes into consideration the welfare of the majority. It is, therefore, a truly egalitarian and democratic principle.

Automatically we maintain within ourselves a concept of an "I", an ego which we hold onto very preciously. For its benefit and for its safety we work. Naturally and spontaneously we wish that this "I" is always happy and never miserable. On this basis we work to gain happiness and to avoid suffering. With this as our aim or motivation, we endeavor to practice a right method for the accomplishment of that goal. We are fully justified in following such a method, and have every right to practice Dharma in order to attain a higher status of rebirth or the definite goodness of nīrvāṇa, the state beyond sorrow.

With exactly the same reason and justification, every single other sentient being in the world from the highest heads of state to the lowliest beggar on the streets of Bangladesh who, if he does not die in the next moment will surely die within an hour, are all completely the same in their desire for happiness which, even though they desire, they lack. Although externally all these beings appear to be different—some living in luxury while others are without anything—they are basically the same in their wish to be free from suffering and their desire to be happy. They are also the same in that they all lack a satisfactory form of happiness. So, when we hold strong preferences between the lowly and the high, because their situation is fundamentally the same from the point of view of them all lacking happiness, we do so without any sensible reason. Therefore, since both rich and poor, powerful and weak strive for happiness and try to avoid misery even though they are totally imbued with it, we must have an equal desire to help them without any distinctions or preferences.

There is an example given in the teachings of my tutor, Kyabje Trijang Rinpoche, that when there are ten beggars who are equally poor, equally lacking in food and equally seeking it, to create a distinction between one and another is quite wrong. They are all in the same situation, all equally seeking help and all equally wishing to be rid of their misery. Likewise, from kings to beggars, no matter what the difference in appearance may be, they are exactly the same in that they all wish not to have any pain and suffering. Yet even though they do not like to suffer, they are actually completely oppressed under its weight. Since this is the same situation for all, to create a difference because of preferences—feeling closer to some and yet distant from others—has no reason or justification at all. Thus, with all our ability, with all our might, we must try to help these beings in an equal way, in an identical manner.

II. The Importance of Others

As I mentioned just before, since all these beings are viewed as equally important in these respects, such a practice and attitude is democratic. However important one may be, one is still only a single being. For instance, with regard to myself, I have the title "Gyalwa Rinpoche" and, having obtained this human body, I have also been ordained as a full monk which is certainly of great value. Moreover, I hold an important title and status so that many people admire me and even praise me. Nonetheless, when I compare myself with others, then no matter how important or valuable I may be, I am but one man. The others are infinite, without limit or end. Even the slightest suffering, when it befalls others, is infinite. The same is true for happiness. When it reaches others, it is infinite. No matter how much happiness one may attain, even the supreme bliss of Buddhahood, it is only for one person. Even though we may have fallen into the most intense suffering of the deepest hell, still only one being will have fallen. It is not a great disaster at all. Only one life will have fallen. Therefore, since others are more important than oneself, it is appropriate to dedicate ourselves to work for the benefit of others. To simply use others for our own welfare is absolutely wrong. As is said in the *Venturing into the Bodhisattva's Way of Life*:

Utilize oneself for others.
To utilize others for oneself is wrong.
There is nothing worse.

Elsewhere it has been said:

If we use everything,
What can we give?
Therefore, considering (the welfare)
of others is a divine practice of Dharma.

Which means that when we use everything for our own purpose, all our possessions and so on, what can we give to others? When instead we start to consider others before ourself, we embark upon a holy practice of Dharma. This text continues:

"If I give, what can I use?"
To think in such a way for oneself
is a diabolical way of the devil.

Which means that to think, "If I give all this, what can I use and gain for myself?" is absolutely demonic.

In brief, if we compare ourself and others, the "others" are infinite. Because they are infinite, because they are the majority, they are more important. This is the way we should meditate.

In conjunction with such texts as the *Venturing into the Bodhisattva's Way of Life*, it was explained to me by the very venerable Khunnu Lama, Tenzin Gyaltsen, that for abandoning lofty thoughts of self-importance, pride and so on we should apply the following methods of meditation. Imagine and visualize on one side of yourself, yourself in your ordinary form. On the other side visualize not all sentient beings, but a group of about fifteen or twenty who are weak and suffering. You should maintain yourself in the middle as an impartial witness between the two. Then project onto your visualized self all your usual selfish qualities and attitudes, so that you identify that self as having all the self-centered characteristics of your body, speech and mind. Then think, "For that one selfish being all these other beings are exploited. For him, all those other sentient beings' benefit and happiness is ignored. He just uses them, taking them for everything he can, just for himself." This, you will feel, is dreadful. That selfish projection of yourself, instead of being concerned for the welfare of this group and trying to help them out of their difficulties, ignores them or, worse still, tries to exploit them for his own selfish ends.

Then we should realize that both the projected negative self on one side and the miserable group on the other are exactly the same. All wish for happiness and freedom from suffering and all have an equal right to attain it. Thus, by keeping a very honest and impartial line as a witness to these two, we will find that the visualized projection of ourself is completely in the wrong. By being honest with ourselves, we must have sympathy for the others and realize just how evil self-centered attitudes are. We will then feel disgusted to find these qualities in ourself and this should bring about a transformation in our mind.

This kind of meditational practice helps nobody other than ourselves. I asked my precious teacher, the Khunnu Lama, Tenzin Gyaltsen, when I received the teaching on the *Venturing into the Bodhisattva's Way of Life*, if this practice was worthwhile and beneficial. He replied that it was very good and highly beneficial. I have found it helpful for my mind so perhaps if you practice it, it may be beneficial for you, as beneficial as practicing the Developing Stage of Highest Yoga Tantra!

III. The Equality of Oneself and Others

There are three basic ways to equalize one's attitude to oneself and others: i) from the side of others, ii) from one's own side and iii) ultimately. There are three aspects within each of those, so there are nine ways involved altogether. As it is said in the practice of *Offering to the Spiritual Master* (bla-ma-mchod-pa; guru-puja) stanza 84:

There is no difference between ourselves and others;
No one wishes even the slightest suffering
Or is ever content with the happiness he has.
Realizing this, we seek your blessings that we may
Enhance the bliss and joy of others.

Oneself and sentient beings are completely the same in desiring happiness and not desiring suffering. With this as a reason we must think deeply that it is worthless to hate someone and to be attached to someone else. Then we must think that although all beings always want to be happy, they all equally lack it. And although none wish for the slightest misery, all are oppressed by it. Just as if there are ten people all equally suffering from an illness, it makes no sense to help just one or two and ignore the others, so it makes no sense to be attached to some beings and to hate or ignore others since they are all equally oppressed by universal suffering. Therefore, we must have the thought applied in our actions of regarding them all equally and benefitting them without any feelings of closeness or distance.

These are the three contemplations from the point of view of others. For oneself there are three things to consider.

Even though from the side of sentient beings it is true to say that since their wish for happiness and avoidance of misery is equal there is no need to feel close to some and distant to others, with regard to oneself, it does seem as though some sentient beings actually are harming while some are truly helping. Perhaps therefore, there is a difference between sentient beings. However, not only are sentient beings equal from the point of view of their own side and aspirations, they are also equal from one's own point of view.

From past lifetimes until now, sentient beings have been of benefit to us innumerable times. Moreover, they will continue to help us over and over again in the future. This being so, we should practice viewing them equally from the point of our own welfare and benefit. Yet we still may think that although they have benefitted us, they have also harmed us, so how can we have an equal attitude? We should put away such doubt. Certainly sentient beings have harmed us in the past but the help they have given far outweighs the harm. If we really compare the help and harm, the help they have given both directly and indirectly, in providing us with our basic necessities of life, is much greater than any harm. Because of this benefit they give to us, we surely must exercise equanimity towards others.

Now we still may hold some doubt about total strangers who have neither helped us nor harmed us. Why should we have an equal respect for these beings? If we do not care for a being because of indifference and because at present we have no direct relationship with him, then we have no reason to be concerned for him. Then even our compassion towards an animal that is about to be slaughtered would be of no sense because it is an object of complete indifference. It has neither helped nor harmed us. However, it is quite appropriate to have compassion for it. If our simplistic reason to be indifferent, to remain impartial and unconcerned because we have no direct involvement with strangers, is sufficient justification for our ignoring them, compassion as a whole is without reason. However, if an animal is suffering, nearly everyone feels compassion towards it. Compassion need not be helped or forced. Just seeing a creature in a poor and difficult situation will cause compassion to arise. It requires no initial help. By thinking in this way, even when sentient beings are not directly helping us, still, because of their miserable situation, we must help them and should be concerned for their welfare.

After this, we may have yet another, stronger doubt. What about enemies who actually do harm us? There must be some difference in our attitude towards them that is reasonably justified. This is absolutely wrong. They are even kinder than the others. This is explained very clearly in the chapter on patience in the *Venturing into the Bodhisattva's Way of Life*.

When an enemy harms us, we can judge if we are a true practitioner of Dharma or not. That which makes the test, the examination of our mental development, is the enemy. When our spiritual masters impart their instructions, it is easy to be a very smart practitioner of Dharma by raising our eyebrows and so on. It is very easy. However, when your so-called enemy points at you and criticizes and blames you saying, "You have done this!" and so on, if your mind at that moment can remain without agitation or reaction, then you are a true practitioner of Dharma. If, instead of remaining in peace, we give a "one for one and two for two" reply, we are not a practitioner of Dharma at all. Thus the enemy is the true yardstick of our inner development.

For instance, these days because of circumstantial changes in time and place I, the Dalai Lama, am almost a simple monk. This is all due to the great kindness of the Chinese uprooting us from our homeland, I do not have to be concerned about my possessions becoming old, decaying or being eaten by moths. Of course, in comparison to when we first arrived in India, we do have a little more. Even the most simple monks now have a key on their belt although they had nothing when they first arrived. Be that as it may, all of us do not have as many things as we had in Tibet. So for myself, compared with before, I have become quite carefree and very simple. If I were in Tibet now, although I would not be a reactionary because I am quite open-minded, and if I were to act as my open mind might wish, some difficulty and problem might arise. Now in another country such complications no longer arise. This is very good. Moreover, even though we Tibetans face many difficulties and problems now, still our minds are not overcome. We can still maintain stability and peace. One important reason for this is because of the many great problems we, as refugees, have already faced and surmounted. Now when some trouble arises we are not defeated by it. This is due to the kindness of the Chinese, who presented us with problems and difficulties. Because we had to overcome them, the mind now is able to resist new hardships.

Therefore, that which gives us problems, causing us harm, difficulties and troubles, that which is conventionally called the "enemy" is in reality a supreme teacher and the best examiner. That which points out directly our emotional afflictions is this supreme guru.

I often tell you stories the Khunnu Lama Rinpoche told me. One such incident was this. One time there was a man circumambulating the main park in Lhasa. On his way he encountered a meditator. The circumambulator asked, "Hey meditator, what are you meditating on?"

He replied, "I'm meditating on patience."

The other then said, "Very well then, eat this filth!"

Immediately the meditator flew into a rage and replied, "Eat it yourself!"

The meditator had told the other man that he was meditating on patience, since that is what his spiritual master had given as his practice. However, the circumambulator was the direct teacher who had come to test his practice by intimidating him with the command, "Eat this filth!" It was he who wanted to make him practice real patience.

In a similar way, when we practice a tantric sādhana or are doing our daily prayers and meditations to the extent that we become very involved, with tears in our eyes, raised eyebrows and so forth, and in the middle are disturbed by some outside noise or are interrupted by a visitor who comes and chatters about nothing in particular so that not even a smell of our practice remains, then hatred, aggression, impatience, attachment and so on all will arise in the mind. Hence it is as has been said: when there is good food and good sunshine, who is a practitioner of Dharma? Yet when unfavorable circumstances befall one, who is an ordinary person?

Therefore, when bad circumstances and difficulties arise, those who are unaffected and who can maintain composure, patience and stability is a true practitioner of Dharma. When bad circumstances occur and one becomes completely overwhelmed with them, just as an ordinary person, one is not at all a practitioner of Dharma. The being who makes this test is the enemy who provokes the arisal of the adverse situation. Consequently there is no one more precious or kind than the enemy. An enemy helps in the elimination and expending of obstacles as well as in the development of patience. If we practice and develop patience, the counterpart—hatred—automatically decreases and weakens. The more this ignoble mind of hatred loses strength, the more the noble mind of virtues like pure love and compassion develops. The more the virtuous mind develops, the stronger bodhicitta becomes, so that this wish to attain the fully awakened state for the benefit of sentient beings will arise and increase. For this reason the enemy becomes very precious..

So of course there is now no question about the beings we feel indifferent toward because we now realize that even our enemies are precious, are the ultimate teachers. Therefore we can never ignore or abandon any sentient being. They have all been infinitely kind to us so we must direct our actions and thoughts into helping them without excluding any.

The third reason why we should regard them all equally is that we are all, ourselves and sentient beings, in exactly the same situation. We are all conditioned in the nature of the suffering of impermanence. As it has been said in the *Venturing into the Bodhisattva's Way of Life*:

> For one who is impermanent to be really attached to
> One who is impermanent is absolutely senseless.

And it continues by saying:

> For one who is impermanent to truly hate
> One who is impermanent is absolutely senseless.

This means that for a being who is subject to the nature of transitoriness, for whom it is even uncertain that he will be alive tomorrow, to be attached or to feel hatred to a being who is equally impermanent is absolutely worthless. For instance, there is no sense in sheep being led to a slaughterhouse to push and fight each other. They are all about to die. This is exactly the same for all of us. Thus there is no sense in being attached to some and to hate others.

This is the third reason why we should feel equal respect towards other beings from our own side. Thus six reasons from the conventional point of view have been covered. There are three more reasons from the ultimate point of view.

If, having contemplated in these ways, the qualm still arises that there really must be friends and enemies—those who help or harm us—and we still feel that we should have a slightly different attitude according to the object, we should then try and view the situation from the ultimate point of view. Since a Buddha is the ultimate example, in what way does he and the Bodhisattvas who are born from his speech see friends and enemies?

As has been said by Āryadeva in *The Four Hundred Stanzas* (bzhi-rgya-pa; Catuḥśataka):

> A doctor is not angry with a patient
> who is possessed by a spirit.
> (In the same way) Buddha sees the emotional
> afflictions themselves, yet not the beings in place of the
> emotional afflictions.

This means that if a person is possessed by a spirit and consequently becomes very angry, shouting at and even attacking the doctor who is trying to help him, the doctor is not angered. He will try to remove the source of the problem from the patient and will not retaliate and become angry. In the same way a Buddha, a Fully Awakened Being, sees all the faults of sentient beings in the light of their mental disturbances and not in terms of sentient beings as being bad. A Buddha therefore sees that all sentient beings, in their nature, are pure, and that all their faults are due to their mental obscurations of conflicting emotions and the traces of these, which prevent the understanding of everything. All blame must be given to these delusions which possess the beings, but not to the sentient beings who have these delusions.

That is the way a Fully Awakened Being sees the situation. Yet we, because we do not realize that all apparently bad characteristics are due to beings' emotional defilements, put all the blame for their faults on the beings themselves. In fact, everything is the fault of the defilements.

Moreover, there is no certainty with friends and enemies. If our enemies were enemies for all time, we would be justified in discriminating between a friend and an enemy. However, as Gung-thang Rinpoche has said:

The friend who is dear to one's heart today,
just by being carried away with projections
due to a few words of difference,
tomorrow can become one's main enemy.

Even from my own experience, leaving aside the changes of several lifetimes, in this very life a friend from my early days can become an enemy in later life, and an enemy in my youth can become a friend when I am an adult. This happens all the time. Therefore, from our own experience we can see that enemies and friends are not permanent. They always change. So to grasp onto a friend as permanent and to think that one's enemies of today will always be so is totally wrong. Even nations once locked in war later become allies. Therefore, with this as our second reason from the ultimate point of view, we must develop an attitude of equally helping others without any differentiation.

The third reason is that friends and enemies are not perceived by the ultimate mind of a Buddha. This does not mean that friends and enemies do not exist conventionally. Friends and enemies do not exist inherently, or just due to their own characteristics. If they do exist inherently, as absolute friends or enemies, then the omniscient mind realizing the ultimate must perceive them. Yet such a distinction is never ultimately perceived and therefore they do not exist inherently. To view things in this way will seriously harm our usual attachments, aggressions and other conflicting emotions, since both subtle and gross mental defilements arise from and are based on ignorance of the lack of inherent existence of all phenomena.

This completes the ninth reason why we must have an equal thought of helping all sentient beings without taking sides and favoring any.

IV. Cherishing Others

Once we have contemplated well and have understood that sentient beings are more important than ourselves, are more precious and that they all should be regarded equally, then, whether beings are kind to us or not, a strong thought of holding other living creatures dearly in our heart will easily arise.

For the creation of this thought of cherishing others it is not necessary that we see how kind other beings have been to us. When we see the suffering of animals for instance, in order for the thought of holding them dear to arise, it is not essential to realize their kindness to us. Just seeing the equality between oneself and them is enough. "If I were in the place of that creature suffering, how could I bear it?" In this way compassion will automatically arise.

For instance, although we do not consider we are being very kind to ourselves, we actually do cherish ourselves most dearly. This does not come as a result of seeing one's kindness to oneself. It just arises naturally. Therefore, just by seeing the equality between ourself and others from the viewpoint that we all are the same in wishing for happiness and wishing to avoid suffering, and then by projecting ourself into the place of others, we will realize from our own experience how they have the same right to these aspirations as we. As much as we desire happiness and hate to be suffering, so do all other sentient beings. By thinking deeply in this way, the thought of cherishing others will automatically arise.

Not only this, we must also meditate deeply on the faults of cherishing ourselves and the excellent virtues of cherishing others. Selfishness is harmful because every single unfortunate circumstance is a result of it. It is like this. We suffer harm fundamentally because we grasp the self-cherishing attitude as something truly existent. This provides the support for selfishness. Moreover even on the high spiritual level of Hīnayāna saints, although they have abandoned grasping at true existence, they still have the self-cherishing thought. Because of this, they fall into one-sided state of passive liberation. In being deceived by subtle thoughts of self-cherishing, their realization becomes limited, lacking the all-encompassing compassion of a Buddha. Every hindrance and bad situation in our own life is due to this self-cherishing attitude. All interferences are its fault. Therefore, as it is explained in the *Offering to the Spiritual Master* by the First Panchen Lama (stanza 85):

> This chronic disease of cherishing ourselves
> Is the cause giving rise to our unsought suffering.
> Seeing this, we seek your blessings to blame, begrudge
> And destroy the monstrous demon of selfishness.

It is like a chronic disease which is both very bad and difficult to root out. It is not like a cold we have for just a few days. It is always present, constantly bothering us, ready to create suffering at the slightest lack of care. It steals our freedom and happiness and always creates trouble.

From beginningless time, throughout all our lives while turning on the wheel of ongoing existence, this attitude of always wishing for "my happiness, my comfort", constantly clinging to oneself as most precious even in dreams, this continual cherishing and grasping of "I, I, I, I" has led to the creation of untold trouble. Therefore this deeply-rooted attitude is a very serious, chronic disease. From the great wars between nations to the quarrelling of two neighbors, all is caused by this.

On the other hand, there is a very great virtue in cherishing other sentient beings. The first Panchen Lama states (stanza 86):

> The mind that cherishes all mother beings and would
> secure
> Them in bliss is the gateway leading to infinite virtues.
> Seeing this, we seek your blessings to cherish these beings
> More than our lives, even should they rise up as enemies.

There is nothing superior to the thought of cherishing and benefiting others, the thought concerned with their welfare and happiness. As sometimes I say (although perhaps I am being controversial but in a way I'm getting to the crux of the matter) that even if one does not believe in reincarnation, it does not matter, and even if one does not believe in the law of actions and their consequences, it may not matter, but for as long as one lives one must maintain a noble and virtuous mind—a good heart and an altruistic attitude. Because, even though one may accept reincarnation completely and understand all the ins and outs of the law of Karma, of what use is such understanding if one keeps a poisonous mind? Someone who knows nothing about such topics, yet keeps a noble and virtuous mind and helps others according to his ability, need have no fear of his rebirth when the time of death comes. It will surely be beneficial. This is what I usually think and say, so that whether or not one accepts doctrines and religious beliefs, the essential practice is to maintain a good heart and to consider others before oneself. If one keeps that state of mind, it is always helpful and most beneficial.

Therefore cherishing other sentient beings is extremely virtuous and has many good qualities. Everything that is positive and wholesome comes from cherishing others through abandoning love of oneself. Temporarily it is pleasant and comforting. Holding others dear brings peace to our mind, expands our outlook and satisfies our immediate needs. Also ultimately, it aids in the cleansing of mental impurities, leading to the accomplishment of total purification of all obstacles, and assists in the accumulation of meritorious goodness leading to the total fulfillment of an Awakened Being's excellent qualities.

Thus, even though we do not intentionally seek for higher or more fortunate rebirths for ourselves, they will automatically arise as a side effect of cherishing others. Moreover, by enhancing the force of acquaintance with these noble and wholesome characteristics of the mind, their good qualities will continue to develop and increase from lifetime to lifetime. As Chandrakīrti has said in his *Supplement to the "Middle Way"* (dbu-ma-la-'jug-pa; Madhya-makāvatara):

> If one develops acquaintance with giving
> through generosity in life and life,
> one will always make connection
> with virtuous spiritual masters.

So cultivating a virtuous mind over lifetimes will also lead us into contact with spiritual guides, who in turn will help us to further develop inner qualities of goodness and virtue. In this way we will gradually accomplish the path.

Therefore, if we can give birth to a mind that cherishes others and endeavors to help them as much as possible, our own welfare and benefit will arise as a side effect. As said by Tsong-kha-pa:

> Never do I hope for the accomplishment of my own purpose. May I always be involved only in accom- plishing the welfare of others.

Thus, even for one's own benefit, this cherishing of others and maintaining a wholesome frame of mind brings comfort to one temporarily and, from the ultimate point of view, leads to the attainment of Buddhahood, beyond which there is nothing greater. Therefore, cherishing other sentient beings is the supreme virtuous attitude.

Every goodness in this world comes from the practice of cherishing others. The great leaders of history, the men who gained fitting respect and wide fame, were mainly concerned with helping in the welfare of others. This they did irrespective of whether such altruistic motivations were an outcome of a specific religion or spiritual doctrine. By this thought of cherishing others, of considering others before themselves, they are now remembered, respected and admired by all people. On the contrary, those leaders who were selfish and only concerned with their own benefit and happiness, even though they may have gained great power in the world, are disliked and scorned by the majority of people. They are spoken of as being evil, selfish and corrupt. For such leaders, this criticism and any punishment they may have received is completely justified. Therefore, it is as is said in the *Offering to the Spiritual Master* (stanza 88):

> Since cherishing ourselves is the doorway to all torment,
> While cherishing our mothers is the foundation of all
> that is good,
> We seek your blessings to make our main practice
> The yoga of exchange of self for others.

Also Śāntideva has said:

> The childish work for their own welfare
> While Buddhas work for the welfare of others.
> Look at this difference.
> What is the need to say more?

From time immemorial the childish have been concerned with their own welfare. What has been the result? What have we gained by this? On the other hand the Buddhas, with the help of spiritual guidance, have totally sacrificed themselves for the welfare of others whom they cherish and hold most dear. They have generated such an attitude and then have embarked on the practices and activities which accord with such a wholesome mind. As a result they have gained total realization and thus have become the refuge and guide of all other beings. Therefore, by realizing this difference between the childish, the spiritually immature, and the enlightened, we must relinquish the self-cherishing attitude and accept the precious thought of cherishing others.

Moreover, Śāntideva explains in the *Venturing into the Bodhisattva's Way of Life*:

> If I cannot completely exchange my happiness
> With the suffering of others, how will it be
> Possible to attain full awakening? Even in
> Cyclic existence I shall find no happiness.

If we cannot put ourselves in the position of others by discarding the wrong attitude of holding ourselves as most important and precious, and if we cannot take on the wholesome attitude of cherishing others, the question of attaining Buddhahood will not be relevant. Even our life within the world will be rent with misery after misery, an ongoing stream of disasters and suffering. On the contrary, if we can dedicate ourselves for the sake of others, holding their welfare as more important, ultimately we shall obtain Buddhahood and temporarily in day-to-day matters of the world we shall be in harmony with others. They will respect and admire us for such qualities.

Thus, although one completely sacrifices and dedicates oneself for the benefit of others without any thought of one's own happiness, one's own welfare and benefit will automatically arise as a result. For this reason we should practice cherishing others as much as we can and should try to see the faults of selfishness so that we can completely vanquish it. As has been concluded by Śāntideva:

> All misery in the world derives from
> Desiring happiness for oneself;
> All happiness of the world arises from
> Desiring the happiness of others.

Which is a wonderful conclusion to reach.

V. Exchanging Oneself with Others

Once our mind has been well-trained in the practice of seeing the faults of self-cherishing and the excellences of cherishing others, the actual exchange of oneself with others will arise.

When we investigate deeply, we will realize that up until now we have looked upon ourselves as the most precious and important. Yet just to consider our own happiness or suffering means nothing. Although we may regard ourselves as very important, such arrogance is nothing. However to make use of ourselves for the sake of others is the very best thing to do. This thought of dedicating oneself totally for the use and service of others must be generated very intensely.

When we say "exchanging oneself with others" it does not mean that one becomes others and others become oneself. What we exchange is this state of mind that considers oneself as the most important and valuable. We direct this attitude to others and the ignoble state of mind which ignores and forsakes others we direct upon ourselves. So when we say "ourself" it is something that does not matter (as we usually think of sentient beings). If we say "others" and they receive happiness for themselves, even at our expense and suffering, we do not worry or mind at all.

"The only purpose of my existence is to be used by others and to serve others." This idea, this attitude, this determination must arise from the depths of one's heart, from the very depths of one's mind.

There is a quotation from Śāntideva that speaks about the wish to be used by all beings just as they use the elements of earth and so forth. As an origin for this quotation Nāgārjuna in the *Precious Garland* itself has said at the end (stanza 483):

> Like the earth, water, fire, wind,
> Medicine and the forests, may I always
> Be a possession commonly used by
> All sentient beings without interference.

Earth, water, fire and air are objects used in common by all living beings. They belong to all. Nobody should claim them as his own. Mountains, forests and places of solitude belong to everyone in common. Like these commonly used objects, we should be determined to sacrifice ourselves for the common benefit of all sentient beings. Such service for others should not be undertaken just for the duration of this life or for a few lifetimes but it should be our resolve to help others for aeons, until the end of time, as far as the reaches of the cosmos, forever. As Śāntideva has said:

> As long as space remains and
> As long as sentient beings remain,
> May I remain with them
> To clear away their suffering.

During that time we must be able to bear however much misery and hardship may befall us in order to carry out our aim of working for the benefit of others. As is said in the *Offering to the Spiritual Master* (stanza 98):

> Even if we must remain for an ocean of aeons in the fires
> Of Avīci Hell even for the sake of just one sentient being,
> We seek your blessings to complete the perfection of
> enthusiastic effort
> To strive out of compassion for Supreme Enlightenment
> without being discouraged.

If, for the fame of attaining Buddhahood quickly in one life or in three years or so, we speak loudly to others about bodhicitta because we hear that it is indispensable to generate it, we are being absolutely wrong. Instead of shouting "Bodhicitta! Bodhicitta!" we should think to ourselves, "If for the benefit and welfare of sentient beings, attaining bodhicitta is essential for attaining Buddhahood, may I therefore generate such a mind." We should not wish to attain Buddhahood in order just to be in a state free from all faults and endowed with all qualities. Nor should we, since we hear that activating the awakening mind is indispensable for such an attainment, go around speaking pretentiously about bodhicitta. To do so is quite wrong. We should discard such an infantile approach and instead must make the firm determination within ourselves to exchange our happiness with the suffering of others. As we say in Tibetan, "From the very depths of our hearts we firmly resolve to exchange ourselves with others. We must transform our thoughts so that we can put ourselves in the position of others." This is called the exchange of self with others.

VI. Giving and Taking

Based on the fundamental thought of exchanging oneself with others, it is taught that we must then practice what is known as "giving and taking". This is a method to increase and develop the power and strength of our mind. In reality the practice of "giving and taking" does not directly clear away the suffering of others, nor does it directly bring them happiness. It is essentially a method of training the mind and developing our skill in the meditations relating to bodhicitta. As is said in the *Seven Point Thought Transformation* (blo-sbyong-don-bdun-ma):

> Practice "giving and taking" entwined.
> Commence the giving from your own side.

We should practice the meditation of taking on ourselves all the suffering that beings may have, and giving them all the happiness and meritorious goodness we have. This we should train in by first relating to ourselves and taking on the suffering that we will experience soon and in the future. This should later be expanded to encompass all living beings.

The main point is to think very deeply about the miserable condition of other sentient beings so that a feeling that cannot bear the suffering of others arises. Then we will reach the point where we think, "Well, what can I do? At the moment sentient beings do not follow ethical conduct, nor do I have the ability to show them a way that will shorten and reduce their suffering." Out of this a strong wish will arise to take on the suffering of others. "May it ripen on me immediately. May I receive all the misery from others." With this strong desire in our hearts we begin the taking. As it says:

> Begin the taking (of suffering) with compassion.

Once all their miseries have been mentally taken on ourselves, we generate a strong wish that all those who lack joy and happiness immediately be endowed with it. Out of this motivation we offer them all merit we have accumulated, imagined in the form of necessities such as clothes for those who need them, healthy physiques for those who are ill or crippled, analytical wisdom for those who require it and so on. Thus, we practice giving as is said:

> Practice giving with pure love.

In this way we should practice "giving and taking". The purpose of doing so is to develop the power of our mind, to strengthen the force of compassion and, as this supreme wish becomes stronger, to activate and enhance the power of the awakening mind.

Conclusion

Practices such as exchanging oneself with others are very beneficial and important, and there is no better instruction than found in Śāntideva's work, the *Venturing into the Bodhisattva's Way of Life*. Of course, if we look at it without some background of texts such as those on the Graded Path (Lam-rim), it may seem a little scattered, but if we are familiar with the order of the Graded Path, it is very beneficial to meditate as is explained in Śāntideva's great work. We should keep this text close to our head, like a pillow, and refer to it again and again. We should also look to the works of Nāgārjuna such as the Precious Garland and pray to be able to realize their complete meaning. Especially refer to the passages explaining the awakening mind and think deeply on them. In this way they will bring some benefit. As it says, "The roots of the awakening mind (should be) firm like Mount Meru, the king of mountains". This precious bodhicitta must be developed until it is firmly integrated in our mind, and this can be done through the Seven Instructions of Causes and their Effect, and through Exchanging Oneself with Others. We must make an effort to do this in accordance with our ability.

Generally for me, although I haven't attained bodhicitta, it is more difficult for me to practice the recognition of mothers. This is because I must think for so long about all my lives—and they are infinite. Thus I make a big jump in my process of meditation to exchanging myself with others, putting myself in their position. I find that from this attitude of cherishing other sentient beings, bodhicitta may come. When this feeling is matured, I no longer dwell on the recognition of mothers. That may gradually come later. This preference is probably due to a difference in disposition. I have a mind which is my own, which has its own ways to develop. Everyone has a different mind and personality. For some, if they practice the meditation of the Seven Instructions of Causes and their Effect, it is more efficient. Whereas for others, the way of Exchanging Self with Others is more effective.

There is a point concerning the remembrance of the kindness of others which is unusual and which I feel should be thought about in depth. It is like this: I think that even though I do not think so much about others' kindness to me, I do cherish and love myself very much. In the same way, instead of helping others by using the reason that they have been so kind to me (which I feel deeply implies an importance of oneself), we should just fully direct our practice towards the fact that they need happiness and must have freedom from suffering. With that reason alone we can develop the attitude of cherishing others. This is what I find.

However, whichever way one practices, it is all according to one's own disposition and characteristics. I am just arranging a number of dishes for you to choose from. If someone likes meat dumplings, meat dumplings are prepared. If some like noodles, noodles are prepared. If some people prefer soup, soup is prepared. I am just explaining to you what I feel. You should take according to what suits your mind and then practice that.

To sum up, from the very depths of our heart we must think, "I must work for the benefit of sentient beings. In order to totally accomplish this aim I must, by all means, attain the complete awakening of Buddhahood. There is no other alternative." With regard to these two thoughts of attaining Buddhahood and of searching for the benefit of sentient beings, I find the former more difficult to arise than the latter. For others, the former is easier and the latter more difficult. This also depends on individual personalities.

Thus the three principles of great compassion, awakening mind and discriminating wisdom realizing emptiness must be practiced by someone aspiring to attain the fully awakened state of Buddhahood. As this verse begins:

> If you and the world wish to attain
> unsurpassable full awakening,
> the root is the awakening mind.

༄༅། །བླ་མ་དང་སྤྱན་རས་གཟིགས་དབྱེར་མེད་

ཀྱི་རྣལ་འབྱོར་དངོས་གྲུབ་ཀུན་འབྱུང་

ཞེས་བྱ་བ་བཞུགས་སོ།

A MEDITATION ON COMPASSION

A Sādhana of the Inseparability of the Spiritual Master and Avalokiteśhvara

by

His Holiness
The Fourteenth Dalai Lama

Translators' Note

Throughout history, man has complained of the degeneration of his times. The present day is no exception. People, rich or poor, powerful or weak, suffer from one form of misery or another. Whether they attempt to confront this reality or withdraw and isolate themselves from it, the suffering of mankind remains. Although war, poverty, disease and mental dissatisfaction continue to plague the world, an individual should never blame others for such problems. The true object of blame for all misfortune is the self-cherishing attitude of those who are directly involved in such confusion. This self-cherishing attitude narrows an individual's outlook to his or her own likes and dislikes and is the motivating force behind the continued creation of his unhappiness.

All beings wish to be happy and free from misery. Although scientific development, modern weapons and abundant material progress may alleviate the temporary effects of dissatisfaction, such external means can never totally eradicate its fundamental cause. The true solution is to cultivate deep human compassion, love and respect for others. Whether a person is a Buddhist or Christian, a follower of a specific religion or simply a believer in non-violence and morality, good human qualities such as kindness, generosity, humility and compassion are preferred by all. By cultivating such altruistic and beneficial attributes, the cause of suffering, self-cherishing, will gradually diminish. This, in turn, will promote unity and harmony among human beings of all nations.

In Buddhist teachings, compassion, the wish that all beings be separated from their suffering, plays an especially important part. In order to help others be free from misery, Buddha taught that the most effective way is to attain the fully purified state Beyond Sorrow (Nirvāna). The wish to do so for the sake of oneself and all others is known as the enlightened motivation of the awakening mind (Bodhicitta). The source of such a selfless motivation is compassion, and its result—accomplished by means of the six transcending perfections (pāramitā): selfless giving, ethics, patience, enthusiastic perseverance, meditative concentration and discriminating awareness—is the full awakening of Buddhahood. In such a state, after completely eliminating every trace of self-cherishing and when directly understanding Voidness, the actual way all things exist, one will become as effective source of benefit for others. This is because an Enlightened Being has the power to lead others out of their suffering.

Although compassion is cultivated in one's own mind, the embodiment of it is the deity known as Avalokiteśhvara (Tib. Chän-rä-zig), the One "Compassionately Regarding the World". The various aspects that are visualized in meditational practices and represented in images and paintings are merely the interpretative forms of Avalokiteśhvara, whereas the actual definitive form is compassion itself. However, the interpretative form is not restricted to meditational deities but can appear in a human form. The Dalai Lamas of Tibet have been recognized as true human manifestations of Avalokiteśhvara. Through his deep compassion he has shown himself in a manner to which one can easily relate. It is fortunate that there is an opportunity to practice this prayer and method for accomplishment (sādhana) written by His Holiness the XIVth Dalai Lama himself.

This sādhana, entitled "The Inseparability of the Spiritual Master and Avalokiteśhvara: a Source of all Powerful Attainments", was composed when His Holiness was nineteen years of age and was first printed in Tibet in the Wood-Horse year (1954). This translation was originally made at the request of Mr. Ang Sim Chai of Malaysia. It is our sincere and deep hope that people, through this practice, will discover a universal means of creating happiness through generating compassion and love for all. May every creature share in its boundless effects.

Grateful acknowledgement is made to those who assisted in this work. The language of the initial rough translation was corrected and improved upon by India Stevens. Thanks also go to Alexander Berzin and Jonathan Landaw for their helpful suggestions.

Sherpa Tulku
B. C. Beresford
Dharamsala
January 1975

༄༅། །རྒྱལ་ཀུན་སྙིང་རྗེའི་རང་བཞིན་བཅུ་དྲུག་ཆ།།
ཡོངས་རྫོགས་བྱིན་རླབས་བདུད་རྩིའི་འོད་དཀར་ཅན།།
བླ་མ་སྤྱན་རས་གཟིགས་ལ་གུས་བཏུད་ནས།།
དེ་ཡི་རྣལ་འབྱོར་ཟབ་མོའི་ཚིག་སྤེལ།།

དེ་ལ་འདིར་བྱིན་རླབས་དང་། དངོས་གྲུབ་ཐམས་ཅད་ཀྱི་རྩ་བ་བླ་མ་ལ་རག་ལས་པར་མདོ་རྒྱུད་དུ་མ་ནས་ལན་གཅིག་མ་ཡིན་པར་བསྟགས་པ་བཞིན་རང་ལ་ལམ་ཕྱིན་ཅི་མ་ལོག་པར་སྟོན་པའི་བླ་མ་དང་ལྷག་པའི་ལྷ་ངོ་བོ་དབྱེར་མེད་དུ་བྱས་ནས་གསོལ་བ་འདེབས་པ་ཉིད་གནད་ཀྱི་མདུན་མའི་གཞི་རྟེན་གཅིག་པུར་གལ་ཆེ་ཞིང་། དེ་ཡང་རང་གང་ལ་མོས་པའི་ཡི་དམ་གྱི་ངོ་བོར་མོས་ཆོག་ཀྱང་། ཐེག་པ་ཆེན་པོའི་ལམ་གྱི་སྲོག་ལྟ་བུ་ནི། བྱམས་སྙིང་རྗེ། བྱང་ཆུབ་ཀྱི་སེམས་རིན་པོ་ཆེ་ཁོ་ན་ཡིན་ཅིང་། སྙིང་རྗེ་ཆེན་པོ་ཐོག་མཐའ་བར་གསུམ་དུ་གལ་ཆེ་བར་གསུངས་པས། རང་གི་རྩ་བའི་བླ་མ་དང་། སྙིང་རྗེའི་ལྷ་མཆོག་འཕགས་པ་སྤྱན་རས་གཟིགས་ཟུང་འབྲེལ་གྱི་རྣལ་འབྱོར་ཉམས་སུ་ལེན་པར་འདོད་པའི་རྣལ་འབྱོར་པས་ཡིད་དུ་འོང་བའི་གནས་སུ་མཆོད་རྫས་སོགས་ལེགས་པར་འདུ་བྱས་ལ། སྟན་བདེ་བ་ལ་འཁོད་དེ། དགེ་སེམས་ཁྱད་པར་ཅན་གྱི་ངང་ནས་སྐྱབས་འགྲོ་སེམས་བསྐྱེད་ཚད་མེད་པ་བཞི་བསྒོམ་པ་སྔོན་དུ་བཏང་།

Introduction

To Avalokiteśhvara, my Spiritual Master, the full moon-like essence
Of the Buddhas' vast compassion and the radiant white nectar
Of their all-inspiring strength, I pay my deep respect.
I shall now disseminate to all other beings the standard practice of this profound yoga.

The root of every inspiration and powerful attainment (siddhi) lies solely with the Spiritual Master (the Lama or Guru). As such he has been praised in both sūtras and tantras[1] more than once. He is of fundamental importance because the basis for achieving everlasting happiness is requesting him to teach the undistorted path. Thinking of him as being inseparable from the specific meditational deity with whom you feel a special affinity, you should visualize the two as one.

The vitality of the Mahāyāna tradition comes from compassion, love and the altruistic aspiration to attain Enlightenment (Bodhicitta) in order to effectively help all creatures become free from their suffering. Moreover, the importance of compassion is emphasized throughout all stages of development. Therefore, if you wish to combine Avalokiteśhvara, the meditational deity of compassion, with your own root Guru, first gather fine offerings in a suitable place. Sitting on a comfortable seat in an especially virtuous state of mind take refuge, generate an enlightened motive of the awakening mind and meditate on the Four Immeasurables.

སྐྱབས་འགྲོ་དང་སེམས་བསྐྱེད།

༄༅། །ན་མོ་གུ་རུ་བྷྱཿ

ན་མོ་བུདྡྷ་ཡཱ།

ན་མོ་དྷརྨ་ཡ།

ན་མོ་སངྒྷ་ཡ།

སངས་རྒྱས་ཆོས་དང་ཚོགས་ཀྱི་མཆོག་རྣམས་ལ།།
བྱང་ཆུབ་བར་དུ་བདག་ནི་སྐྱབས་སུ་མཆི།།
བདག་གི་སྦྱིན་སོགས་བགྱིས་པའི་བསོད་ནམས་ཀྱིས།།
འགྲོ་ལ་ཕན་ཕྱིར་སངས་རྒྱས་འགྲུབ་པར་ཤོག །

ཚད་མེད་པ་བཞི།

སེམས་ཅན་ཐམས་ཅད་བདེ་བ་དང་བདེ་བའི་རྒྱུ་དང་ལྡན་པར་གྱུར་ཅིག །

སེམས་ཅན་ཐམས་ཅད་སྡུག་བསྔལ་དང་སྡུག་བསྔལ་གྱི་རྒྱུ་དང་བྲལ་བར་གྱུར་ཅིག །

སེམས་ཅན་ཐམས་ཅད་སྡུག་བསྔལ་མེད་པའི་བདེ་བ་དང་མི་འབྲལ་བར་གྱུར་ཅིག །

སེམས་ཅན་ཐམས་ཅད་ཉེ་རིང་ཆགས་སྡང་དང་བྲལ་བའི་བཏང་སྙོམས་ལ་གནས་པར་གྱུར་ཅིག ། (ལན་གསུམ།)

Preliminaries

I. Refugee Formula

Namo Gurubhyah	In the Spiritual Masters I seek refuge,
Namo Buddhāya	In the Awakened One I seek refugee,
Namo Dharmāya	In his Truth I seek refuge,
Namo Saṅghāya	In the Spiritual Aspirants I seek refuge.

II. The Generation of the Enlightened Motive

In the Supreme Awakened One, His Truth
and the Spiritual Community,
I seek refuge until becoming Enlightened.
By the merit from practicing giving
and other perfections,
May I accomplish Full Awakening
for the benefit of all.

III. The Four Immeasurables

May all sentient beings possess happiness
and the cause of happiness.
May all sentient beings be parted from suffering
and the cause of suffering.
May all sentient beings never be parted from
the happiness that has no suffering.
May all sentient beings abide in equanimity without
attachment or aversion for near or far.

(Recite these prayers three times each.)

༡ ཐམས་ཅད་དུ་ནི་ས་གཞི་དག །
གསེག་མ་ལ་སོགས་མེད་པ་དང་།།
ལག་མཐིལ་ལྟར་མཉམ་བཻ་ཌཱུར་ཡའི།།
རང་བཞིན་འཇམ་པོར་གནས་གྱུར་ཅིག །
ལྷ་དང་མི་ཡི་མཆོད་པའི་རྫས།།
དངོས་སུ་བཤམས་དང་ཡིད་ཀྱིས་སྤྲུལ།།
ཀུན་བཟང་མཆོད་སྤྲིན་བླ་ན་མེད།།
ནམ་མཁའི་ཁམས་ཀུན་ཁྱབ་གྱུར་ཅིག །

ཨོཾ་ན་མོ་བྷ་ག་ཝ་ཏེ། བཛྲ་ས་ར་པྲ་མརྡ་ནེ་ཏ་ཐཱ་ག་ཏཱ་ཡ། ཨརྷ་ཏེ་སམྱཀྶཾ་བུདྡྷཱ་ཡ། ཏདྱ་ཐཱ། ཨོཾ་བཛྲེ་བཛྲེ། མཧཱ་བཛྲེ། མཧཱ་ཏེ་ཛ་བཛྲེ། མཧཱ་བིདྱཱ་བཛྲེ། མཧཱ་བོ་དྷི་ཙིཏྟ་བཛྲེ། མཧཱ་བོ་དྷི་མཎྜོ་པ་སཾ་ཀྲ་མ་ཎ་བཛྲེ། སརྦ་ཀརྨ་ཨཱ་ཝ་ར་ཎ་བི་ཤོ་དྷ་ན་བཛྲེ་སྭཱ་ཧཱ། (ཞེས་ལན་གསུམ་བརྗོད།)

དཀོན་མཆོག་གསུམ་གྱི་བདེན་པ་དང་། སངས་རྒྱས་དང་བྱང་ཆུབ་སེམས་དཔའ་ཐམས་ཅད་ཀྱི་བྱིན་གྱི་བརླབས་དང་ཚོགས་གཉིས་ཡོངས་སུ་རྫོགས་པའི་མངའ་ཐང་ཆེན་པོ་དང་། ཆོས་ཀྱི་དབྱིངས་རྣམ་པར་དག་ཅིང་བསམ་གྱིས་མི་ཁྱབ་པའི་སྟོབས་ཀྱིས་དེ་བཞིན་ཉིད་དུ་གྱུར་ཅིག ། (ཅེས་ས་གཞི་དང་། མཆོད་རྫས་བྱིན་གྱིས་བརླབས། དེ་ནས།)

Actual Practice

I. Purification

May the surface of the Earth in every direction
Be stainless and pure, without roughness or fault,
As smooth as the palm of a child's soft hand
And as naturally polished as lapis lazuli.[2]

May the material offerings of gods[3] and of men,
Both those set before me and those visualized
Like a cloud of the peerless offerings of Samantabhadra,[4]
Pervade and encompass the vastness of space.

OM NAMO BHAGA-VATE VAJRA-SARA PRA-MARDA-NE TATHA-GATA-YA ARHA-TE SAMYAK-SAM-BUDDHA-YA TADYA-THA OM VAJRE VAJRE MAHA-VAJRE MAHA-TEJRA VAJRE MAHA-VIDYA VAJRE MAHA-BODHICITTA VAJRE MAHA-BODHI-MAN-DOPA SAMKRAMA-NA VAJRE SARVA-KARMA AVARA-NA VISHO-DHANA VAJRE SVA-HA. *(Recite this purification mantra three times.)*

By the force of the truth of the Three Jewels of Refuge,
By the firm inspiration from all Bodhisattvas and Buddhas,
By the power of the Buddhas who have fully completed
Their collections of both good merit and insight,
By the might of the Void, inconceivable and pure,
May all of these offerings be hereby transformed
Into their actual nature of Voidness.

(In this way bless the surroundings and the articles of offering.)

༡ བདེ་ཆེན་ལྷུན་གྲུབ་ཆོས་སྐུའི་མཁའ་དབྱིངས་སུ།།
སྣ་ཚོགས་ཀུན་བཟང་མཆོད་སྤྲིན་འཁྲིགས་པའི་དབུས།།
།སེང་གེས་བཏེགས་པའི་འོད་འབར་ནོར་བུའི་ཁྲིར།།
ཆུ་སྐྱེས་ཉི་ཟླ་རྒྱས་པའི་གདན་སྟེང་དུ།།
སྙིང་རྗེའི་གཏེར་ཆེན་འཕགས་མཆོག་འཇིག་རྟེན་དབང་།།
རྣམ་པ་དུར་སྨིག་འཆང་བའི་གློས་གར་ཅན།།
རྩ་བའི་བླ་མ་གསུམ་ལྡན་རྡོ་རྗེ་འཛིན།།

རྗེ་བཙུན་བློ་བཟང་བསྟན་འཛིན་རྒྱ་མཚོའི་དཔལ།།
དཀར་དམར་མདངས་གསལ་དགྱེས་པའི་འཛུམ་ཞལ་ཅན།།
ཕྱག་གཡས་ཐུགས་ཀར་ཆོས་འཆད་ཕྱག་རྒྱ་ཡིས།།
གླེགས་བམ་རལ་གྲིས་མཚན་པའི་པད་དཀར་དང་།།
གཡོན་པ་མཉམ་གཞག་རྩིབས་སྟོང་འཁོར་ལོ་བསྣམས།།
གུར་ཀུམ་མདངས་ལྡན་ཆོས་གོས་རྣམ་གསུམ་དང་།།
བཙོ་མའི་གསེར་མདོག་པཎ་ཞྭ་མཛེས་པར་གསོལ།།

ཕུང་ཁམས་སྐྱེ་མཆེད་ཡུལ་དང་ཡན་ལག་རྣམས།།
རིགས་ལྔ་ཡབ་ཡུམ་སེམས་དཔའ་སེམས་མ་དང་།།
ཁྲོ་བོའི་རང་བཞིན་དཀྱིལ་འཁོར་འཁོར་ལོར་རྫོགས།།
སྣ་ལྔའི་འོད་ཕྲེང་འཁྲུགས་པའི་གུར་ཁྱིམ་དབུས།།

II. Visualization

In the space of the Dharmakāya[5]
of great spontaneous bliss,
In the midst of billowing clouds
of magnificent offerings,
Upon a sparkling jewelled throne
supported by eight snow lions,[6]
On a seat composed of a lotus in bloom,
the sun and the moon,[7]
Sits supreme Exalted Avalokiteśhvara,
great treasure of compassion,
Assuming the form of a monk
wearing saffron-colored robes.

O my Vajradhāra Master, kind in all three ways,[8]
Holy Lozang Tenzin Gyatso,
Endowed with a glowing fair complexion
and a radiant smiling face,
Your right hand at your heart
in a gesture expounding Dharma
Holds the stem of one white lotus
that supports a book and sword,[9]
Your left hand resting in meditative pose
holds a thousand-spoked wheel.[10]
You are clothed in the three saffron robes of a monk,[11]
And are crowned with the pointed,
golden hat of a Paṇḍit.[12]

Your aggregates, sensory spheres, senses,
objects and your limbs
Are a maṇḍala complete with
the Five Buddhas and their consorts,[13]
Male and female Bodhisattvas
and the wrathful protectors.
Encircled by a halo of five brilliant colors,[14]

ཞབས་གཉིས་མི་ཕྱེད་རྡོ་རྗེའི་སྐྱིལ་དཀྲུང་ཚུལ།།
གང་འདུལ་སྒྱུ་འཕྲུལ་དྲྭ་བའི་སྤྲིན་ཕུང་འགྱེད།།

ཐུགས་ཀར་ཡེ་ཤེས་སེམས་དཔའ་སྤྱན་རས་གཟིགས།།
ཞལ་གཅིག་ཕྱག་བཞིའི་དང་ཟུང་ཐལ་མོ་སྦྱར།།
འོག་མས་ཤེལ་ཕྲེང་པདྨ་དཀར་པོ་བསྣམས།།
རིན་ཆེན་རྒྱན་དང་དར་གྱི་ན་བཟས་མཛེས།།
རི་དྭགས་པགས་པས་ནུ་མ་གཡོན་པ་བཀབ།།
ཟླ་བའི་ལང་ཚོ་པད་ཟླར་སྐྱིལ་ཀྲུང་བཞུགས།།
དེ་ཡི་ཐུགས་ཀར་ཏིང་འཛིན་སེམས་དཔའ་ནི།།
ཧྲཱིཿཡིག་དཀར་གསལ་འོད་ཟེར་ཕྱོགས་བཅུར་འཕྲོ།།

བླ་མའི་གནས་གསུམ་རྡོ་རྗེ་གསུམ་གྱིས་མཚན།།
ཐུགས་ཀའི་ཧཱུྃ་ཡིག་ལས་འཕྲོས་འོད་ཟེར་གྱིས།།
རབ་འབྱམས་མཆོག་གསུམ་མ་ལུས་སྤྱན་དྲངས་ཏེ།།
ཐིམ་པས་སྐྱབས་གནས་ཀུན་འདུས་ངོ་བོར་གྱུར།།

(ཅེས་བླ་མ་སེམས་དཔའ་སུམ་བརྩེགས་ཀུན་འདུས་ནོར་བུའི་ལུགས་སུ་གསལ་གདབ།)

My master is seated in full vajra posture,
Sending forth a network of cloud-like
self-emanations
To tame the minds of all sentient beings.

Within his heart sits Avalokiteśhvara,
a wisdom being,[15]
With one head and four arms.
His upper two hands are placed together,
His lower two hands hold a crystal rosary and
white lotus.[16]
He is adorned with jewelled ornaments and
heavenly raiment.
Over his left shoulder an antelope skin is draped,[17]
And cross-legged he is seated on a silver moon and lotus.[18]
The white syllable HRIH ཧྲཱིཿ, a concentration being
at his heart,
Emits brilliant colored light in all the ten directions.

On my Master's brow is a white OM ༀ,
within his throat, a red AH ཨཱཿ,
At his heart, a blue HUM ཧཱུྃ, from which
many lights shine out in myriad directions,
Inviting the Three Jewels of Refuge
to dissolve into him:
Transforming him into the collected essence
of the objects of refuge.

(In this manner visualize the Spiritual Master.)

༡ གསལ་རྫོགས་མཚན་དཔེས་མཛེས་པའི་མཐོང་གྲོལ་སྐུ།།
སྙན་འཇེབས་དྲུག་ཅུའི་དབྱངས་ལྡན་འགག་མེད་གསུང་།།
ཟབ་ཡངས་མཁྱེན་བརྩེ་དཔག་པར་དཀའ་བའི་ཐུགས།།
གསང་གསུམ་རྒྱན་གྱི་འཁོར་ལོར་གུས་ཕྱག་འཚལ།།

བདག་པོས་བཟུང་དང་མ་བཟུང་མཆོད་པའི་རྫས།།
དངོས་བཤམས་ཡིད་སྤྲུལ་ལུས་དང་ལོངས་སྤྱོད་དང་།།
དུས་གསུམ་བསགས་པའི་རྣམ་དཀར་དགེ་ཚོགས་ཀུན།།
ཀུན་བཟང་མཆོད་སྤྲིན་རྒྱ་མཚོར་དམིགས་ནས་དབུལ།།

མ་རིག་འཐིབ་པོའི་སྨག་གིས་ཡིད་ནོན་པས།།
བཅས་རང་ཁ་ན་མ་ཐོའི་སྡིག་ལྟུང་སོགས།།
ལོག་པར་འཕྱུན་པའི་ཉོངས་པ་ཅི་མཆིས་པ།།
འགྱོད་སྡོམ་དྲག་པོས་དམིགས་མེད་ངང་དུ་བཤགས།།

དཔལ་ལྡན་བླ་མའི་རྣམ་པར་ཐར་པ་དང་།།
ཐེག་གསུམ་སྐྱེ་འཕགས་རང་གཞན་ཐམས་ཅད་ཀྱི།།
དུས་གསུམ་རྣམ་དཀར་དགེ་བའི་ཕུང་པོ་ལ།།
སྙིང་ནས་བསམ་པ་ཐག་པས་རྗེས་ཡི་རང་།།

III. The Seven-Limb Prayer

Prostrating

Your liberating body is fully adorned with
all the signs of a Buddha;[19]
Your melodious speech complete with all
sixty rhythms flows without hesitation;
Your vast profound mind filled with wisdom
and compassion is beyond all conception;
I prostrate to the wheel of these three secret
adornments of your body, speech and mind.

Offering

Material offerings of my own and of others,
The actual objects and those that I visualize,
Body and wealth, and all virtues amassed
throughout the three times,
I offer to you upon visualized oceans
of clouds like Samantabhadra's offerings.

Confessing

My mind being oppressed by the stifling darkness of ignorance,
I have done many wrongs against reason and vows.
Whatever mistakes I have made in the past,
With a deep sense of regret I pledge never to repeat them
And without reservation I confess everything to you.

Rejoicing

From the depths of my heart I rejoice
In the enlightening deeds of the sublime Masters
And in the virtuous actions past, present and future
Performed by myself and all others as well,
And by ordinary and exalted beings of the
Three Sacred Traditions.[20]

སྣ་ཚོགས་གདུལ་བྱའི་ཁམས་ཀྱི་རྗེས་སོང་པའི།།
དམ་ཆོས་སྐབས་གསུམ་ལྷ་ཡི་རོལ་མོའི་སྒྲ།།
ཟབ་ཞིའི་དབྱིངས་སུ་འཁྲོལ་བས་ཡིད་ཅན་ཀུན།།
ཤེས་ཉོན་སྒྲིབ་པའི་གཉིད་ལས་སློང་དུ་གསོལ།།

སྲིད་ཞིའི་མུ་མཐའ་བྲལ་བའི་མངོན་རྟོགས་ལ།།
འགྲོ་ཀུན་བདེ་བའི་དབུགས་འབྱིན་མ་ཐོབ་བར།།
ཞབས་ཟུང་ཨེ་ཝཾ་མི་ཤིགས་སྐྱིལ་མོ་ཀྲུང་།།
གཡོམ་མེད་རྡོ་རྗེའི་ཁྲི་ལ་བརྟན་པར་བཞུགས།།

རྣམ་དཀར་ལེགས་བྱས་བགྱིས་དང་བགྱིད་འགྱུར་ཀུན།།
རྗེ་བཙུན་བླ་མས་འབྲལ་མེད་རྗེས་འཛིན་ཅིང་།།
ཀུན་བཟང་སྤྱོད་མཆོག་སྨོན་ལམ་ཡོངས་འགྲུབ་ནས།།
འགྲོ་ཀུན་དོན་དུ་རྫོགས་བྱང་ཐོབ་ཕྱིར་བསྔོ།།

༩ ས་གཞི་སྤོས་ཀྱིས་བྱུགས་ཤིང་མེ་ཏོག་བཀྲམ།།
རི་རབ་གླིང་བཞིའི་ཉི་ཟླས་བརྒྱན་པ་འདི།།
སངས་རྒྱས་ཞིང་དུ་དམིགས་ཏེ་དབུལ་བར་བགྱི།།
འགྲོ་ཀུན་རྣམ་དག་ཞིང་ལ་སྤྱོད་པར་ཤོག །

Requesting

I request you to awaken every living being
From the sleep of ordinary and instinctive defilements
With the divine music of the Dharma's pure truth,
Resounding with the melody of profoundness and peace
And in accordance with the dispositions of your
various disciples.

Entreating

I entreat you to firmly establish your feet
Upon the indestructible vajra throne
In the indissoluble state of E-WAM,[21]
Until every sentient being gains the calm breath of joy
In the state of final realization, unfettered by the
extremes of worldliness or tranquil Liberation.

Dedicating

I totally dedicate my virtuous actions of all the three times
So that I may receive continuous care from a Master,
And attain Full Enlightenment for the benefit of all,
Through accomplishing my prayers,
the supreme deed of Samantabhadra.

IV. *The Maṇḍala Offering*

By directing to the Fields of Buddhas
This offering of a maṇḍala built on a base,
Resplendent with flowers, saffron water and incense,
Adorned with Mount Meru and the four continents,
As well as the sun and the moon,
May all sentient beings be led to these Fields.

བདག་གཞན་ལུས་ངག་ཡིད་གསུམ་ལོངས་སྤྱོད་དུས་གསུམ་དགེ་ཚོགས་དང་།།
རིན་ཆེན་མཎྜལ་བཟང་པོ་ཀུན་བཟང་མཆོད་པའི་ཚོགས་དང་བཅས།།
བློ་ཡིས་བླངས་ནས་བླ་མ་ཡི་དམ་དཀོན་མཆོག་གསུམ་ལ་འབུལ།།
ཐུགས་རྗེའི་དབང་གིས་བཞེས་ནས་བདག་ལ་བྱིན་གྱིས་བརླབ་ཏུ་གསོལ།།
ཨི་དཾ་གུ་རུ་རཏྣ་མཎྜལ་ཀཾ་ནི་རྱཱ་ཏ་ཡཱ་མི།།

(ཞེས་ཡན་ལག་བདུན་པ་མཎྜལ་དང་བཅས་པ་འབུལ།)

༥ རྗེ་བཙུན་བླ་མའི་ཐུགས་ཀའི་ཧྲཱིཿཡིག་ལས།།
བདུད་རྩི་འོད་ཟེར་སྣ་ལྔའི་རྒྱུན་བབས་ཏེ།།
རང་གི་སྤྱི་བོ་ནས་ཞུགས་སྡིག་སྒྲིབ་སྦྱང་།།
མཆོག་ཐུན་དངོས་གྲུབ་མ་ལུས་ཐོབ་པར་གྱུར།།(ཅེས་བརྗོད་ཅིང་བསམས་ལ།)

ཨོཾ་ཨཱཿགུ་རུ་བཛྲ་དྷ་ར་ཝཱ་གིནྡྲ་སུ་མ་ཏི་ཤཱ་ས་ན་དྷ་ར་ས་མུ་དྲ་སརྦ་སིདྡྷི་ཧཱུྃ་ཧཱུྃ།

(ཞེས་མཚན་སྔགས་གང་འགྲུབ་བཟླ། དེ་ནས་འདོད་བྱའི་དོན་ལ་གསོལ་བ་འདེབས་པ་ནི།)

༦ འཕྲལ་དང་ཡུན་གྱི་བདེ་བ་མ་ལུས་པའི།།
གཞིར་གྱུར་མ་ནོར་ལམ་སྟོན་དྲིན་ཅན་རྗེ།།
རབ་འབྱམས་སྐྱབས་ཀྱི་ཕུང་པོར་ངེས་རྙེད་ནས།།
བསམ་སྦྱོར་དག་པས་བསྟེན་པར་བྱིན་གྱིས་རློབས།།

This offering I make of a precious jewelled maṇḍala,
Together with other pure offerings and wealth
And the virtues collected throughout the three times
With body, speech and mind.

O my Masters, my Yidams[22] and the Three Precious Jewels,
I offer all to you with unwavering faith.
Accepting these out of your boundless compassion,
Send forth to me waves of your inspiring strength.
Om Idam Guru Ratna Maṇḍalakam Niryata Yami

(Thus make the offering of the Maṇḍala together with the Seven-Limb Prayer.)

V. The Blessing by the Master

From the HRIH ཧྲཱིཿ in the heart of Avalokiteśhvara,
Seated in the heart of my Venerable Master,
Flow streams of nectar and rays of five colors
Penetrating the crown of my head,
Eliminating all obscurations and endowing me with both
Common and exclusive powerful attainments.

OM AH GURU VAJRADHARA VAGINDRA SUMATI SHASANA DHARA SAMUDRA SHRI BHADRA SARVA SIDDHI HUM HUM

(Recite the mantra of the Spiritual Master as many times as possible.)

VI. The Prayer of the Graduated Path

Bestow on me your blessings to be devoted to my Master
With the purest thoughts and actions, gaining confidence
that you,
O compassionate holy Master, are the basis of temporary
and everlasting bliss,
For you elucidate the true Path free from all deception,

ནོར་མཆོག་བྱེ་བས་བསྒྲུན་མིན་དལ་འབྱོར་རྟེན།།
ཐོབ་ཀྱང་མི་བརྟན་ནམ་འདོར་ཆ་མེད་པས།།
འདི་སྣང་བྱ་བས་ནམ་ཡང་མི་གཡེང་བར།།
དམ་ཆོས་སྤྱོད་པས་འདའ་བར་བྱིན་གྱིས་རློབས།།

བཟོད་དཀའ་ངན་འགྲོའི་འཇིགས་ལས་སྐྱོབས་པའི་ཕྱུལ།།
མཆོག་གསུམ་གཏན་གྱི་སྐྱབས་སུ་ལེགས་བཟུང་སྟེ།།
དཀར་ནག་ལས་འབྲས་ཇི་བཞིན་སེམས་པ་ཡིས།།
སྡིག་སྤོང་དགེ་སྒྲུབ་ནུས་པར་བྱིན་གྱིས་རློབས།།

སྲིན་མོའི་བསླུ་བྲིད་ཇི་བཞིན་ལྷ་དབང་གི །
ཕུན་ཚོགས་ཀུན་ཀྱང་བསླུ་བའི་ཆོས་ཅན་དུ།།
མཐོང་བའི་ངེས་འབྱུང་དྲག་པོས་རྒྱུད་བསྐུལ་ནས།།
བསླབ་གསུམ་ཉམས་ལེན་བྱེད་པར་བྱིན་གྱིས་རློབས།།

ཐོག་མེད་དུས་ནས་དྲིན་གྱིས་ལེགས་བསྐྱངས་པའི།།
ངང་ཚུལ་བསམས་ནས་སེམས་མཆོག་རབ་བསྐྱེད་དེ།།
སྲིད་ཞིའི་རྒུད་པས་མནར་བའི་མར་གྱུར་འགྲོའི།།
སྤྱོད་པ་རྒྱ་མཚོར་སློབ་པར་བྱིན་གྱིས་རློབས།།

And embody the totality of refuges past number.
Bestow on me your blessings to live a life of Dharma
Undistracted by illusory preoccupations of this life,
For well I know that these leisures and endowments
Can never be surpassed by countless treasures of vast wealth,
And that this precious form once attained cannot endure,
For at any moment of time it may easily be destroyed.

Bestow on me your blessings to cease actions of non-virtue
And accomplish wholesome deeds by being always mindful
Of the causes and effects from kind and harmful acts,
While revering the Three Precious Jewels as the ultimate
source of refuge
And the most trustworthy protection from the unendurable fears
Of unfortunate rebirth states.

Bestow on me your blessings to practice the three
higher trainings,[23]
Motivated by firm renunciation gained from clear
comprehension
That even the prosperity of the Lord of the Devas[24]
Is merely a deception, like a siren's alluring spell.

Bestow on me your blessings to master the oceans of practice,
Cultivating immediately the supreme Enlightened
Motivation,
By reflecting on the predicament of all mother sentient beings,
Who have nourished me with kindness from
beginningless time
And now are tortured while ensnared within one
extreme or other,
Either on the wheel of suffering or in tranquil Liberation.

རབ་དྭངས་གཡོ་མེད་མཉམ་གཞག་མེ་ལོང་ངོགས།།
མཐའ་བྲལ་གདོད་ནས་སྟོང་པའི་ངོ་མཚར་འབུམ།།
འགོག་མེད་བཀྲ་བའི་ཞི་ལྷག་ཟུང་འབྲེལ་གྱི།།
རྣལ་འབྱོར་རྒྱུད་ལ་སྐྱེ་བར་བྱིན་གྱིས་རློབས།།

མཚན་ལྡན་རྡོ་རྗེ་འཛིན་པའི་བཤེས་གཉེན་གྱི།།
དྲིན་ལས་ཆོས་ཟབ་སྔགས་ཀྱི་སྒོར་ཞུགས་ནས།།
དངོས་གྲུབ་རྩ་བ་དམ་ཚིག་སྡོམ་པ་རྣམས།།
ཚུལ་བཞིན་བསྲུང་བར་ནུས་པར་བྱིན་གྱིས་རློབས།།

གཉིས་མེད་བདེ་སྟོང་ཡེ་ཤེས་མཚོན་རྟེན་གྱིས།།
ཀུན་བྱེད་ལས་རླུང་རྒྱུ་བ་རབ་བཅད་ནས།།
སྐུ་ཐུགས་ཟུང་འཇུག་བདེ་ཆེན་ཕྱག་རྒྱ་ཆེ།།
ཚེ་འདིར་མངོན་དུ་འགྱུར་བར་བྱིན་གྱིས་རློབས།།

(།ཞེས་མདོ་སྔགས་ཀྱི་ལམ་ཡོངས་རྫོགས་རྒྱུད་ལ་སྐྱེ་བའི་གསོལ་འདེབས་དང་བཤར་སྒོམ་བྱས་མཐར་བླ་མ་སྙིང་ཞུགས་དང་འབྲེལ་བར་ཡིག་དྲུག་གི་བཟླས་པ་བྱ་བ་ནི།)

༥ །དེ་ལྟར་གསོལ་བ་བཏབ་པས་བླ་མ་མཆོག །
།དགྱེས་བཞིན་བྱོན་ཏེ་རང་གི་ཚངས་བུག་བརྒྱུད།།
།འདབ་བརྒྱད་སྙིང་དབུས་མི་ཤིགས་ཐིག་ལེར་ཐིམ།།
།དེ་སྙིང་སྣར་ཡང་པད་ཟླར་བླ་མའི་སྐུ།།

Bestow on me your blessings to generate the yoga
Combining mental quiescence with penetrative insight,
In which the hundred thousand-fold splendor of Voidness,
    forever free from both extremes,[25]
Reflects without obstruction in the clear mirror of the
    immutable meditation.

Bestow on me your blessings to observe in strict accordance
All the vows and words of honor that form the root of
    powerful attainments,
Having entered through the gate of the extremely
    profound Tantra
By the kindness of my all-proficient Master.

Bestow on me your blessings to attain within this lifetime
The blissful Great Seal of the Union of Body and Wisdom,[26]
Through severing completely my all-creating karmic energy
With wisdom's sharp sword of the non-duality of Bliss
    and Voidness.[27]

Having made requests in this way for the development in your mind-stream of the entire paths of Sutra and Tantra, and thus having done a glance meditation on them, now recite the six-syllable mantra in connection with the merging of the Spiritual Master into your heart.

VII. The Merging of the Spiritual Master

My supreme Master, requested in this way,
Now blissfully descends through the crown of my head
And dissolves in the indestructible point
At the center of my eight-petalled heart[28]
Now my Master re-emerges on a moon and lotus,
    in his heart sits Avalokiteśhvara,
Within whose heart is the letter HRIH ཧྲཱིཿ

སེམས་དཔའ་སུམ་བརྩེགས་སྣར་བཞིན་གསལ་བ་ཡི།།
ཐུགས་ཀའི་ཧྲཱི༔མཐར་ཡིག་དྲུག་སྔགས་ཕྲེང་གིས།།
བསྐོར་ལས་བདུད་རྩིའི་རྒྱུན་བབས་ནད་གདོན་དང་།།
སྡིག་སྒྲིབ་ཀུན་བྱང་ལྷུང་རྟོགས་ཡོན་ཏན་རྒྱས།།
སྲས་བཅས་རྒྱལ་བའི་བྱིན་རླབས་མ་ལུས་ཐོབ།།
སླར་ཡང་འོད་འཕྲོས་སྣོད་བཅུད་སྨིན་སྦྱངས་ཏེ།།
སྣང་གྲགས་རིག་གསུམ་འཕགས་པའི་གསང་གསུམ་དུ།།
འཁྱེར་བའི་རྣལ་འབྱོར་མཆོག་ལ་གནས་པ་གྱུར།།

(ཅེས་བརྗོད་ཅིང་བསམས་ལ། ཡིག་དྲུག་ཅི་ནུས་སུ་བཟླ། ཨོཾ་མ་ཎི་པདྨེ་ཧཱུྃ། མཐར་ཡི་གེ་བརྒྱ་པས་བརྟན་པར་བྱས་ལ།)

ཨོཾ། བཛྲསཏྭ། སམཡ། མནུཔཱལཡ། བཛྲསཏྭ། ཏྭེནོཔཏིཥྛ། དྲྀཌྷོམེབྷཝ། སུཏོཥྱོམེབྷཝ། སུཔོཥྱོམེབྷཝ། ཨནུརཀྟོམེབྷཝ། སརྦསིདྡྷིམྨེཔྲཡཙྪ། སརྦ་ཀརྨ། སུཙམེ། ཙིཏྟཾ། ཤྲིཡཾ། ཀུརུཧཱུྃ། ཧཧཧཧཧོཿ བྷགཝན། སརྦཏཐཱགཏ། བཛྲ མམེམུཉྩ། བཛྲཱིབྷཝ། མཧཱསམཡསཏྭ། ཨཱཿ ཧཱུྃ་ ཕཊ།

༤ འདིས་མཚོན་ལེགས་བྱས་ཟླ་གཞོན་འབུམ་གྱི་གཟིས།།
བློ་གཏེར་རྒྱལ་བའི་ཆོས་ཚུལ་ཀུནདའི་ཚལ།།
བཤད་སྒྲུབ་གེ་སར་དགོད་པས་ས་ཆེན་ཁྱེན།།
ཞིས་པ་སྒྲུབ་པས་སྲིད་མཐར་མཛེས་གྱུར་ཅིག །

Encircled by a rosary of the six-syllable mantra,
the source from which streams of nectar flow,
Eliminating all obstacles and every disease
And expanding my knowledge of the scriptural
and insight teachings of the Buddha.
Thus I receive the entire blessings
Of the Victorious Ones and their Sons,
And radiant lights again shine forth
To cleanse away defects from all beings and their environment.
In this way I attain the supreme yogic state,
Transforming every appearance, sound and thought
Into the three secret ways of the Exalted Ones.[29]

After completing the above, recite the six-syllable mantra, OM MAṆI PADME HUM, as many times as possible. Upon conclusion recite once the hundred-syllable mantra of Vajrasattva.

OM VAJRASATTVA SAMAYA MANU PALAYA, VAJRASATTVA TVENO PATISHTA, DIRDHO ME BHAVA, SUTOSHYO ME BHAVA, SUPOSHYO ME BHAVA, ANU RAKTO ME BHAVA, SARVA SIDDHAM ME PRAYACCHA, SARVA KARMA SUCHA ME, CITTAM SHRIYAM KURU HUM, HA HA HA HA HOH, BHAGAVAN SARVA TATHAGATA, VAJRA MA ME MUNCA, VAJRA BHAVA, MAHA SAMAYA SATTVA, AH HUM PHAT.

VIII. Dedication

In the glorious hundred thousand-fold radiance
of the youthful moon of wholesome practice,
From the blue jasmine garden of the Victorious
Treasure Mind's method of Truth,[30]
May the seeds of explanation and accomplishment
germinate and flower across this vast earth;
May the ensuing auspiciousness beautify everything
until the limit of the universe.[31]

ཕུན་ཚོགས་དགེ་ལེགས་བྱེ་བས་རབ་བརྗིད་པའི།།
དགའ་ལྡན་ཆབ་སྲིད་ནོར་བུའི་རྒྱལ་མཚན་ཆེ།།
མི་ནུབ་སྲིད་གསུམ་ཟླ་ན་སྒྲེང་པ་ཡིས།།
ཕན་བདེའི་འདོད་པ་འབུམ་དུ་འཇོ་གྱུར་ཅིག །

རྒྱ་ཆེན་དབྱིག་འཛིན་སྣེག་མོའི་ཁྲིན་ཡངས་པོར།།
དུས་ཀྱི་རྒུད་པའི་མུན་ཚོགས་ཐག་བསྲིངས་ནས།།
བདེ་སྐྱིད་སྣང་བ་དར་བའི་དགེ་མཚན་ཆེར།།
ཡིད་ཅན་རྣམ་པར་རྩེན་པས་སྐྱེམས་གྱུར་ཅིག །

མདོར་ན་སྐྱེ་བའི་ཕྲེང་བར་མགོན་ཁྱོད་ཀྱིས།།
འབྲལ་མེད་མཉེས་བཞིན་རྗེས་སུ་བཟུང་བའི་མཐུས།།
ཀུན་གྱི་དབང་ཕྱུག་ཟུང་འཇུག་རྒྱལ་ས་ཆེར།།
འབད་མེད་བདེ་བླག་ཉིད་དུ་སོན་གྱུར་ཅིག །

(ཅེས་བསྔོ་བ་བྱ་ཞིང་། གཞན་ཡང་བཟང་པོ་སྤྱོད་པའི་སྨོན་ལམ་སོགས་བསྔོ་བ་སྨོན་ལམ་ཅི་རིགས་པའི་མཐར།)

མཇུག་བསྡོམས།

སྲས་བཅས་རྒྱལ་བའི་རྨད་བྱུང་ཐུགས་རྗེའི་མཐུས།།
ཕྱོགས་དུས་ཀུན་ཏུ་མི་མཐུན་རྒུད་ཚོགས་ཞི།།
སྲིད་ཞིའི་དགེ་ལེགས་ཡར་ངོའི་ཟླ་བ་ལྟར།།
འཕེལ་རྒྱས་དགེ་མཚན་དར་བའི་བཀྲ་ཤིས་ཤོག །

By flying high above the three realms[32]
The never-vanishing great jewelled banner of religious
and secular rule,[33]
Laden with millions of virtues and perfect accomplishments,
May myriad wishes for benefit and bliss pour down.

Having banished afar the dark weight of this era's
degeneration,
Across the extent of the earth—a sapphire held by a
celestial maiden—
May all living creatures overflow with spontaneous gaiety
and joy
In the significant encompassing brilliance of happiness
and bliss.

In short, O protector, by the power of your affectionate care,
May I never be parted from you throughout the rosaries
of my lives.
May I proceed directly, with an ease beyond effort,
Unto the great city of Unification, the all-powerful cosmic
state itself.[34]

Having offered prayers of dedication in this way, also recite others such as the "Yearning Prayer of Samantabhadra's Activity" or "The Prayer of the Virtuous Beginning, Middle and End".[35] Upon conclusion recite the following prayer.

Conclusion

By the force of the immaculate compassion of the
Victorious Ones and their Sons,
May everything adverse be banished for eternity
throughout the universe.
May all favorable omens become increasingly
auspicious,
And may whatever is of virtue in the round of this
existence or in tranquil Liberation
Flourish and grow brighter like a new moon waxing full.

ཅེས་ཤེས་པ་བརྗོད་པས་མཐའ་བརྒྱན་པར་བྱའོ།། ཞེས་པ་འདི་ཡང་དད་སྟོབས་ལྷག་བསམ་དགེ་བ་བཀའ་བློན་ལས་རོགས་ཤན་ཁ་བ་འགྱུར་མེད་བསོད་ནམས་སྟོབས་རྒྱལ་ནས། ངོས་དང་སྤྱན་རས་གཟིགས་དབྱེར་མེད་ཀྱི་བླ་མའི་རྣལ་འབྱོར་ལམ་ཡོངས་རྫོགས་ཀྱི་བཤར་སྒོམ་མདོར་བསྡུས་ཚང་ཞིང་། མཚན་སྔགས་དང་། ཡིག་དྲུག་གི་བཟླས་པ་ཡང་བྱས་ཆོག་པ་ཆ་ཚང་ཁྱེར་བདེ་ཞིག་དགོས་ཞེས་བདོག་པའི་རྟེན་དང་བཅས་ནན་ཏན་ཆེན་པོས་བསྐུལ་བར། རང་གིས་རང་ལ་འདི་ལྟ་བུའི་རྣལ་འབྱོར་སྦྱར་བ་མི་རིགས་ཀྱང་། དད་པ་བྱས་ན་ཁྱི་སོར་རིང་བསྲེལ་འབྱུང་བ་ལྟར། སློབ་མའི་ངོས་ནས་མོས་གུས་བྱུང་ན་སོ་སྐྱེ་ལས་ཀྱང་སངས་རྒྱས་ཀྱི་བྱིན་རླབས་འབྱུང་བས། དད་ལྡན་འགའ་ཤས་ལ་དོན་དུ་འགྱུར་བ་སྲིད་སྙམ་སྟེ། པད་དཀར་འཆང་བའི་མིང་འཛིན་ཤཱཀྱའི་དགེ་སློང་ངག་དབང་བློ་བཟང་བསྟན་འཛིན་རྒྱ་མཚོས་སྦྱར་བའོ།། །

This has been written at the repeated request of the assistant Cabinet Minister, Mr. Shankawa Gyurme Sonam Tobgyal, who with sincere faith and offerings, asked me to write a simple and complete sādhana of the inseparability of Avalokiteśhvara and myself. This devotion contains a short glance meditation on the entire Graduated Path and the mantras of the Master and Avalokiteśhvara. Although it is improper for me to write such a devotion about myself, waves of inspiration of the Buddhas can be received from ordinary beings just as relics can come from a dog's tooth.[36] *Therefore, I have composed this with the hope of benefiting a few faithful disciples.*

The Buddhist monk
Ngawang Lozang Tenzin Gyatso
maintaining the title of
Holder of the White Lotus
(Avalokiteśhvara)

Notes

1. The sūtras are teachings of Buddha dealing with general subjects while the tantras concern esoteric matters.
2. Lapis lazuli is a semi-precious gem, deep blue in color and usually highly polished.
3. "Gods" are those beings who abide in the celestial realms, the rebirth state with the least suffering within the cycle of existence (saṃsāra).
4. Samantabhadra is one of the eight Bodhisattvas of the Mahāyāna lineage. He is famed for the extensiveness of his offerings made to the Buddhas of the ten directions.

   "Bodhisattva" literally means "Courageously Minded One Striving for Enlightenment". A Bodhisattva courageously endures any hardship to overcome ignorance and the momentum of previous unskillful actions in order to attain Full Enlightenment for the benefit of all other beings.
5. The Dharmakāya is the Truth Body of a Fully Enlightened Being. It is the final accomplishment of all practices and results from an accumulation of meditational insight.
6. Four of the eight snow lions look upwards providing protection from interferences from above. Four gaze downwards protecting from those below.
7. The lotus, rising through the mire of a swamp, symbolizes the purity of the Bodhisattva who rises above the bonds of cyclic existence, uncontaminated by the confusion of the world. The moon symbolizes the conventional Enlightened Motivation of Bodhicitta: the altruistic aspiration to attain Buddhahood for the sake of others. The sun symbolizes the ultimate Wisdom of Bodhicitta: the direct cognition of Voidness, the true mode of existence.
8. "Vajradhāra Master" is a name given to a Tantric Master, indicating that he is considered inseparable from Buddha Vajradhāra (Tib. Dorje Chang, Holder of the Vajra Scepter), the tantric emanation of Buddha Shākyamuni. The Vajra is a symbol of strength and unity. He is kind in three ways by giving the empowerment to practice the deity yoga of Tantra, the oral transmission that remains unbroken from the Enlightened One himself, and the oral explanation of the tantric procedures based on his own experience.
9. The white lotus symbolizes the pure nature of the discriminating wisdom of penetrative insight into Voidness. The knowledge of this is symbolized by the

book of scripture resting on the lotus together with the flaming sword of total awareness that cuts through the root of ignorance. The scripture is one of the "Perfection of Wisdom" (Prajñāpāramitā) sūtras.

10. The thousand-spoked wheel signifies the turning of the Wheel of Truth (Dharmacakra), the teachings of the Buddha.
11. The three robes stand for the three higher trainings in ethics, meditative stabilization and discriminating wisdom.
12. The golden hat of a Paṇḍit symbolizes pure morality. Its pointedness stands for penetrative wisdom. A Paṇḍit is a master of the five major branches of knowledge: art, medicine, grammar, reasoning and the inner or Buddhist sciences.
13. Meditation on the Five Buddhas, or Conquerors (Jina), is utilized in tantric practice to purify the five aggregates (skandha) and to transform the five defilements of greed, hatred, self-importance, jealousy and ignorance into the five wisdoms. The five aggregates are form, feeling, recognition, compositional factors and consciousness. The five wisdoms are of voidness, equality, individuality, accomplishment and the mirror-like wisdom. The Five Conquerors are often mentioned in translations as "Dhyani Buddhas".
14. The five colors are red, blue, yellow, green and white. They are associated with the Five Buddhas.
15. A wisdom being (ye-shes sems-pa) is the actual implied being in one's visualization of a deity. Initially, in visualization, one creates conceptually out of a relaxed but controlled imaginative concentration a mentally manifested being (dam-tsig sems-pa). This creation eventually merges with the wisdom being when one's vision of the deity becomes non-conceptual.
16. The beads on the crystal rosary held by Avalokiteþvara symbolize sentient beings. The action of turning the beads indicates that he is drawing them out of their misery in cyclic existence and leading them into the state Beyond Sorrow (Nirvāṇa). The white lotus symbolizes his pure state of mind.
17. The antelope is known to be very kind and considerate towards its offspring and is therefore a symbol for the conventional Enlightened Motivation, the cultivation of a kind and compassionate attitude towards others.
18. The moon stands for the method by which one follows the spiritual path and engages in the conduct of the Bodhisattvas. The lotus symbolizes the discriminating wisdom of insight into Voidness.
19. There are thirty-two major and eighty minor signs that indicate the attainments of an Enlightened Being.
20. The Three Sacred Traditions of Buddhism are those of the Śrāvakas, Pratyekabuddhas and Bodhisattvas.
21. E-WAM is a Sanskrit seed syllable meaning "thus". It symbolizes the unity of the positive and negative aspects of cosmic energy which, in terms of the momentum from the past and the potentiality of the future, are unified in the present.
22. The Yidam is the meditational deity with whom one identifies when practicing tantric deity yoga. This should only be done after having received empower-

ment from a fully qualified Tantric Master.

23. The three higher trainings (śhīkṣas) are ethics (śhīla), meditative concentration (samādhi) and discriminating wisdom (prajñā).
24. Even Indra, the Lord of the Devas, will one day expend the accumulation of virtuous actions that cause him to hold one of the highest positions within the six realms of cyclic existence, and he too will fall into a lower realm.
25. The two extremes are the beliefs in either true self-existence or non-existence. The Middle Way (Madhyamaka) shows a path that is neither of these.
26. The Great Seal (mahāmudrā, phyag-rgya chen-po) of the Union of Body and Wisdom (yuganaddha, zung-'jug) is the unity of the clear light (prabhāsvara, 'od-gsal) and the illusory body (mayakāya, sgyu-lus), The illusory body is the finest physical body, a combination of energy (vāyu, rlung) and consciousness (citta, sems). The clear light is the wisdom of the non-duality of Bliss and Voidness.
27. The non-duality of Bliss and Voidness is the bliss of the direct understanding of Voidness.
28. The heart wheel (cakra) of the central psychic channel (nāḍī) has eight divisions.
29. The three secret ways of the Exalted Ones are viewing all surroundings as a blissful abode (maṇḍala) and all beings as manifestations of deities, hearing all sound as mantra and intuitively knowing everything to be empty of true existence.
30. "Victorious Treasure Mind" is a name given to Mañjuśṛī, the meditational deity embodying discriminating wisdom. His method of Truth is the direct cognition of Voidness.
31. The limit of the universe is when all beings attain Full Enlightenment.
32. The three realms are the realms of desire, form and formlessness.
33. Religious and secular rule refers to the form of government in Tibet prior to 1959.
34. The great City of Unification, the all-powerful cosmic state, is Buddhahood.
35. "Bhadracaryāpraṇidhāna" (bzang-po spyod-pa'i smon-lam) is the "Yearning Prayer of Samantabhadra's Activity". "Thog-mtha'-ma" by rJe Tsong-kha-pa is "The Prayer of the Virtuous Beginning, Middle and End".
36. Once in Tibet a very devout woman asked her son, who journeyed on trading expeditions to India, to bring back for her a relic of Buddha. Although the son went three times, each time he forgot the promised relic. Not wanting to disappoint his mother again, he picked up a dog's tooth as he was nearing home on his last journey and reverently presented that to her. She was overjoyed and placed the tooth upon the family altar. She then made many devotions to the "holy tooth" and, to the amazement of her son, from the tooth came several true relics.